THE COMIC SPIRIT IN
GEORGE MEREDITH

THE COMIC SPIRIT

IN

GEORGE MEREDITH

AN INTERPRETATION

BY

JOSEPH WARREN BEACH

New York

RUSSELL & RUSSELL

CONTENTS

NOTE

THE Author is indebted to the courtesy of Messrs. Constable & Company, of London, and Messrs. Charles Scribner's Sons, of New York, for permission to use the various short extracts from George Meredith's works printed in this volume.

THE COMIC SPIRIT IN
GEORGE MEREDITH

CHAPTER I

THE COMIC SPIRIT

My aim in this book is to trace in Meredith's novels the comic spirit that makes their chief distinction. This aspect of his work has been much ignored by the critics. In their preoccupation with his amazing style, with his Shakespearean women, with his philosophic message, they have neglected what is for me the very "open sesame" to the treasure house. They never fail to pay perfunctory tribute to Meredith's wit and humor. But the comedy itself they pass by with grave unconsciousness; or they pause to name it, as in duty bound, only to proceed with nervous haste.[1] This is the more

[1] There are exceptions, particularly in the last few years. There is a chapter on the Comic Spirit in J. A. Hammerton's "George Meredith in Anecdote and Criticism," Mitchell Kennerley, 1909. Richard H. P. Curle has chapters on the Comic Spirit and the Sense of Humour in his "Aspects of George Meredith," Routledge, 1908. James Moffatt frequently mentions the Comic Spirit in his Meredith "Primer" (Hodder and Stoughton, 1909), especially in the Introduction. This work had not come to my attention until after the completion of my study; nor had the excellent work of Constantin Photiadès ("George Mere-

1

surprising in view of the many passages in which
the author discusses the nature of comedy, and
the frequency with which he applies the term
to his own novels. Not only does he describe
three of the novels explicitly as comedies, and
designate as "tragic comedians" the leading
characters of another book.[1] But, aside from
frequent allusions throughout the novels and
poems,[2] Meredith has a set treatise on comedy in

dith," etc., Librairie Colin, Paris, 1910). I have not yet
seen the German study of Meredith by Dr. Ernest Dick.
Perhaps the best discussion of Meredith in relation to
comedy that I have seen is in an article by Edmund Gosse
in the "International Monthly," Sept., 1901, entitled
"The Historic Place of Mr. Meredith and Mr. Hardy."
But references to the comic spirit in Meredith are mostly
fleeting and fragmentary, and the critics seem always in
haste to leave this subject.

[1] "Evan Harrington," III: "Our comedy opens with
his return from Portugal." XLIV: "This is a comedy, and I
must not preach lessons of life here."   XXXVIII: "So
ends the fourth act of our comedy."   Compare the reference to the Comic Muse in the beginning of XIV. In
"Sandra Belloni," XLIV, the author refers to "our people
in this comedy"; in I, he speaks of the danger of his
comedy's bordering on the burlesque if he should sketch
portraits of the Pole ladies. The "Egoist" is designated
in the title as "A Comedy in Narrative." In the "Tragic
Comedians," besides the title, consider passages in the
prefatory chapter and in chapters XVIII and XIX.

[2] See in the poems especially the "Spirit of Shakespeare" and the "Two Masks," besides the "Ode to the
Comic Spirit." In the novels, besides the passages referred to in the footnote above, references to comedy and
the comic spirit will be found in "Richard Feverel," chap-
ter-heads to XI and XXIX; "Sandra Belloni," chapter-
head to XXVI, and in XV and XLII; "Rhoda Fleming,"
XXVIII, XXXII; "Vittoria," XX, XL; "Beauchamp,"
XXV; "Egoist," prelude and XXXVII; "Diana," I, XI;

the prelude to the "Egoist"; and he has published
both a lecture on "Comedy" and an "Ode to the
Comic Spirit." No writer since Ben Jonson has
given plainer advertisement of what he was about.
And yet the comic method of Meredith was in
some ways so new, and he used the word comedy
in a sense so unfamiliar to contemporary English
readers, that they have not understood his intention. It has not often occurred to the critics to
extend the application of the word comedy beyond "Evan Harrington" and the "Egoist."
Outside these novels, they find the comic merely

"Lord Ormont," XX; "Amazing Marriage," XL, also
XVII; "The Gentleman of Fifty," I. I have not attempted to make this an exhaustive list, nor have I
included in it passages in which the word *comic* appears as an adjective just synonymous with *funny*. In
"Celt and Saxon" there is an interesting paragraph in
chap. VI on "grisly humour" akin to tragedy, in which
light is thrown on the nature of comedy. I have omitted
reference to the innumerable passages in which the word
humor is used. It may be interesting to note that Meredith attributes a sense of humor not merely to his heroines Vittoria, Janet, Ottilia, Clara, Diana, Nesta and Alice
Amble, but also to Lady Jocelyn, Lady Pluriel and Lady
Charlotte Eglett, the Margravine, Julia Bulsted, Madge
Winch, the "Honest Lady" of the Enamoured Sage; to the
Countess de Saldar, Mrs. Lupin, Mrs. Waddy; to Adrian
Harley and Evan Harrington, Jack Raikes, Agostino Bal-
derini, Homeware, Richmond Roy, Squire Beltham, Baske-
lett and Colney Durance, Everard Romfrey, Sir Willoughby Patterne, Vernon Whitford, Doctor Middleton,
Gower Woodseer; to Luigi the spy, Alphonse the cook, the
Italian revolutionaries and the English people! On the
function of laughter in general, something will be said in
the next chapter.

in such drolls as Mrs. Chump and Master Gammon. I believe that, in Meredith's own view, the comic spirit has just as striking manifestations in such a serious character as Victor Radnor; that no novel of Meredith is quite free from it; and that most of them it pervades like an atmosphere.[1]

In his famous "Essay," Meredith was not so much reviewing the practice of the comic art as attempting to shadow forth the method on which he was at work himself. His effort to illustrate his meaning was somewhat pitiful. He could cite a few instances of comic writing in English literature; but in quoting from "Jonathan Wild," he must draw on his own imagination for the instance, mistaking it for memory. Somewhat vain is his effort to find the comic in Congreve. He would have been more intelligible

---

[1] The comic spirit is not confined to the novels. Very interesting is its manifestation in the poems. I need only name a few titles to suggest how pervasive it is: "Grandfather Bridgeman," the "Beggar's Soliloquy," "A Stave of Roving Tim," "Juggling Jerry," the "Old Chartist," "Jump-to-Glory Jane," the "Empty Purse." You may find the comic spirit in the "Ballads and Poems of Tragic Life"; you may find it in "Modern Love," in the "Ballad of Fair Ladies in Revolt," in the "Sage Enamoured and the Honest Lady." But, after all, it is a spirit without a body that appears in the poems: we do not find the comic types of character which are my chief concern in this book; and a discussion of this phase of my subject is a luxury I cannot allow myself at present.

had he drawn his illustrations from his own novels. He must have been sore tempted to do so. One might suppose that the "Egoist," which appeared two years after the lecture was delivered, was offered to show what he had in mind.

Taking humor as an inclusive term for all varieties of the ludicrous,[1] we may distinguish two functions of humor. The primary function is to make one laugh, the secondary function is to make one think. With most English humorists, the primary function has prevailed, largely to the exclusion of the secondary. With Meredith the secondary function is all-important. He would make us laugh to make us think. Or rather, he would make us smile, and that not always with the muscles of eye and mouth, but inwardly. Meredith would reserve the terms comic and comedy for humor that is addressed to the mind. He would not apply them to those works of humor which are controlled by feeling, whether the bitter feeling of the satirist or the rosily genial sentiment of the humorist proper.

[1] In reference to literature, Meredith generally uses the words humor and humorist (which he does not spell this way) in the more restricted sense, applying them to such writers as Dickens, Sterne, Carlyle, to productions of what I call below "fat humor."

Juvenal and Jonson are beneath his notice; and
equally likewise Sterne and Dickens. He will
not mention these by name, nor admit acquaintance with them. His comedy is "humor of the
mind."

His comedy is hard to define. This butterfly
still eludes our wheel, and flutters away into
regions of uncharted air. If one might venture
to pin it down with a vulgar metaphor? There
is humor and there is lean humor. Meredith's
comedy is lean humor. It is humor divested of
those appurtenances of the sensuous, of sentimentality, of naturalistic detail, of material accident, of waggish impertinent wit, that make so
fat and succulent the work of most English
humorists. I do not mean that Meredith is
wanting either in wit or in human sympathy.
He is a famous master of epigram, and com-
mands a most frolicsome fancy, fertile in all
manner of drolleries. But, save in his earliest
works, these are instruments under strict control of the comic idea, and they are not indulged
wantonly for their own sake. As for humanity,
the characters upon whom he turns the most
searching light of ridicule are shown the gentle
indulgence of one who has taken a wide survey
of human nature, and who feels the force of that

saying, "*que tout comprendre c'est tout pardonner.*"
And nothing equals the tender sweetness with
which he treats his Richards and Lucys, his
Emilias and Carinthias. But this is very different from the familiar and "larmoyant geni-
ality" in which the humorist wades, and which
has no purpose beyond the sensation of the
moment. Meredith has ever in mind the more
thoughtful and fruitful method of comedy, whose
aim is the correction of folly.

The game of all humorists is folly. But the
comic spirit hunts the follies of men and women
in society: of the intelligent, the cultivated, the
urbane,—those who have leisure from pressing
physical needs: that leisure, as Voltaire puts it,
"in which men, left to themselves, abandon
themselves to their characters, and become ridiculous." [1] High comedy deals with high life.
This phrase may be taken literally or in the
ordinary sense, and is equally applicable to
Meredith's *dramatis personæ.* Meredith is not
concerned with those lower strata of society in

[1] From his sketch of the life of Molière. Speaking of the
time of production of "L'Étourdi," Voltaire says: "La
bonne comédie ne pouvait être connue en France, puisque
la société et la galanterie, seuls sources du bon comique, ne
fesaient que d'y naître. Ce loisir dans lequel les hommes
rendus à eux-mêmes se livrent à leur caractère et à leur
ridicule, est le seul temps propre pour la comédie."

which vice and suffering have so debased as to
make unrecognizable the divine features of man.
Debased humanity has nothing to teach us.
Disease and crime are for the doctor. Intelligent, clean, respectable men are the subject of
comedy, which has no interest in Sairey Gamp
or Chevy Slyme. This is not a matter of social
rank. Fletcher's Mirabel and Vanbrugh's Sir
John Brute are quite as foreign to the self-respect-
ing genius of comedy. Among the best lies the
hope for mankind, and it is there one finds the
foibles and cunning vices that are at once most
diverting and most instructive.

Meredith's characters are chiefly drawn, moreover, from the higher degrees of social rank, and
represent high life in the special sense. His
comic figures in particular are prone to flourish
titles. From the entrance of the Countess de
Saldar to the retirement of the Earl of Fleetwood, we find ourselves in distinguished company. This is not, I think, a betrayal of aristocratic tastes on the part of the Radical author,
a desire to adorn his pages with titles that should
bestow an artificial lustre. Comedy makes
choice of persons wealthy and high in rank because here the comic traits of character have
freest play. It would be hard to find in a society

not aristocratic an intelligent and witty person in whom vanity and egoism had a chance to develop so freely as in Sir Willoughby Patterne. Richmond Roy and Victor Radnor could not have indulged their foolish ambitions without command of large sums of money. The comic spirit gives them rope.

But, we must observe, true comedy does not consist in the exploitation of originals. It is urged in behalf of Dickens that his characters are transcribed from real life. Dickens needs not this apology. His figures are droll and graphic,—the work of a genius in charcoal. No one can approach him in his own field. But the oddity of an eccentric is no lesson to men in society. There is no significance in Captain Cuttle's hook or Admiral Trunnion's patch. These appeal to the eye for laughter; they have no message to the mind.

Meredith is in contrast with the humorists in this respect, that his more humorous characters are not those he is hunting. It is the serious characters that are comic. Sterne and Dickens summon us to the enjoyment of persons whom we cannot conceive as related to ourselves, though we recognize in them an amplification of universal human traits. We might take them,

like Don Quixote, for comic symbols of humanity. We can afford to welcome and caress them.
Whimsical, good-hearted fellows appeal to us for
laughter at their odd and captivating ways.
Nick Bottom and Justice Shallow we relish
hugely, looking down upon them. In the company of Dickens and Smollett, we have the
pleasure of laughing to scorn the hypocrite, the
uncharitable, the grossly affected among us.
Meredith invites us to the anatomy of ourselves.

Not even the author's favorites are wholly
exempt from the comic inquisition. The comic
spirit is an atmosphere, completely enveloping
the group in view. It is possessed of chemical
properties, and infallibly attacks any soluble
matter with which it comes in contact. Thus
we find it at work upon certain weak spots in
the character of young Evan Harrington. Evan
Harrington is inevitably associated with Meredith himself: son of a tailor, but endowed
with the instincts of a gentleman. Oneself
is the last person upon whom one turns the
light of comedy. In the "Egoist" our sympathy is chiefly solicited for Clara Middleton
and Vernon Whitford; but we read one chapter
in which "the comic muse has an eye on" these
"two good souls." And the most favored of all

the author's heroines are often conducted on the way with some touch of sympathetic but mildly patronizing drollery.

In four places Meredith informs us explicitly of the function of the comic spirit.[1] Always he is a hunter, an executioner, an agency of correction and discipline. We learn, for example, that comedy "watches over sentimentalism with a birch rod." Comedy is not hostile to honest feeling, but to that false sentiment that turns its back on truth and prefers to bask in the rose-pink light of illusion. The sentimentalist is more concerned to cushion himself against hard fact than to train himself for encountering it. He lives upon sweetmeats and intoxicants. He drugs himself against the perception of truth.

Such is the game the comic spirit delights in. Under various disguises that spirit masquerades, now appearing as the Philosopher, now as Common Sense. Now his name is legion, and he seems a leash of wicked imps eager to be after the prey. It is ever the same spirit. To each act and thought of each character is applied a

[1] The Essay "On the Idea of Comedy and the Uses of the Comic Spirit," first delivered as a lecture in 1877; the Prelude to the "Egoist"; the "Ode to the Comic Spirit"; and the "Two Masks."

powerful solvent, that breaks down every false element in the composition.

This comic analysis is very different from what we have in George Eliot, though she too displays the scientific genius of the day in minute observation of psychological fact. She often accompanies the thoughts of her characters with a dry humor, a mild sarcasm and irony that partake of the comic spirit. But Meredith's pagan serenity has a very different effect from the anxious, high-strung morality of Mary Ann Evans.[1] Her main object is to present studies in right and wrong, in the bettering or debasement of character. She is an evangelical: to her the name for mistaken conduct is sin. Meredith is not concerned with saints and sinners, but with the natural and the unnatural, the honest and the dishonest, those who know their own minds and the victims of delusion. His appeal is not so much to the conscience as to the judgment. He asks for an exercise of imagination in the discovery of our own folly.

[1] In Harry Richmond, XXXII, Meredith catches himself in a fit of epigrammatic moralizing quite in the manner of George Eliot ("We are sons of yesterday, not of the morning. The past is our mortal mother, no dead thing," etc.); and he apologizes: "My English tongue admonishes me that I have fallen upon a tone resembling one who uplifts the finger of piety in a salon of conversation."

George Eliot analyzes characters to this extent, that she displays their motives and their progress in grace or dishonor. There is little of the comic essence in this. It is the discrepancy between the real and the supposed motive that makes the comedy; the game of bluff played by the actor against himself, his complacent self-deception, his mock sublimity.

This is the heart of Meredith's comic method, what distinguishes him among comic writers. The incongruity that is the basis of the ludicrous in general is here found within a man's very soul. Meredith is not content to make laughter from the exhibition of those obvious discrepancies between character and profession, those glaring vanities, simplicities and hypocrisies that have occupied a Fielding and a Thackeray. He insists on sounding the depths for comedy. We read chapter heads like these: "We descend into a steamer's engine-room"; "We take a step to the centre of egoism." We learn, "the twists of the heart are the comedy." Meredith deals with persons not comic on the surface, and shows them to be comic by the exhibition of their inner life. One character is comic because of the discrepancy between the passion on which he prides himself and the factitious sentiment he harbors. One,

upon investigation, proves to be the primitive
egoist mistaking himself for a social being.

Thus we are taught to recognize ourselves.
Cultivated, respectable,—incapable of gross affectation or misdemeanor: we learn that our most
cherished ideals are often based upon false esti-
mates of value; that our very refinement has
sometimes carried us beyond the reach of common sense.

The mere presentation of comic types is not
comedy. This art requires that a character
should be presented in its social relations. Sir
Roger and Mr. Micawber, these are portraits,
framed and stationary on the wall, loved for
their own endearing features apart from any
comic action. Comedy judges character by its
reactions, by the style of gait and bow as the
chosen gentleman walks through the figures of
the minuet. "The Comic Spirit conceives a
definite situation for a number of characters";
and the development of this situation is followed
by a broad search-light of irony.

Dramatic irony might be described as an
oblique light thrown upon some remark by the
circumstances of the play,—a light the more
comic or tragic for not being observed by the
speaker himself. The remarks of Polonius are

full of comic irony, as where he says of Hamlet's satirical hits upon himself, "Though this be madness, yet there is method in it." But the meaning of the word irony may be much extended. In the finest comedy we have a large and pervasive irony, which constitutes the very central comic idea. In high comedy, there is always some suggestive contrast or opposition of character to character, or of character to environment; some squinting light of ridicule cast on one character by another or by the circumstances of the story.

The classic example of this sort of contrast is Molière's "Misanthrope." "Célimène is worldliness: Alceste is unworldliness." And the opposed extremes of plain-dealer and coquette illuminate one another with reciprocated mockery. A social paradox is their juxtaposition; their conjunction would mean explosion. "The School of Wives" is interesting in relation to Meredith's first novel for a situation throwing reflections upon a theory,—a System. It is further interesting as dealing with a system involving injustice to women. Almost every comedy of Meredith involves some judgment upon men for their selfish and mistaken treatment of women. In "The School of Wives," the old-fashioned Arnolphe puts in practice his oriental theory of seraglio-isolation. He boasts to his friend of the ignorance and simplicity which he has carefully fostered in the young woman whom he is raising for his own consumption. But this simplicity proves to be a mask under which the clever Agnès plays her comedy of deceit. Her guardian is ingeniously made go-between of the young lovers, the very instrument of his own undoing. When at last the grieved and bewildered man demands of his ward why she will not love him, she replies with telling justness: "Why have you not made me love you as he did?" And when he twits her with want of gratitude for her careful bringing-up, she replies with ironical praise of a system that would have made her a fool. Alas! he had taken such a pride in his system!

Jane Austen has some telling instances of comic irony: as the scene in which Darcy proposes to Elizabeth, and feels it necessary to apologize to her for this reluctant surrender to passion. This whole story, with its fine contrast of characters, is comedy of a rare conception. Meredith himself refers to "Emma" for the light of irony that falls on the mistaken assumptions and miscarrying plots of the heroine.

But the most striking examples of this large irony may be taken from Meredith himself. We find in him situations of moving seriousness, set forth with masculine vigor and incisiveness. He has a much greater range of vision than was possible for a maiden lady of limited experience. The comic irony is not confined to droll situations involving the amorous sentiment of young people, but throws its reflections more broadly upon the big and grave concerns of men. Thus in "Sandra Belloni," the kid-glove fastidiousness, the sentimental "fine shades" of the Pole sisters are subtly comic in view of the financial embarrassment that more and more threatens to undermine and blow up their flimsy social structure. In "One of Our Conquerors," the obstinate and perverse optimism of the leading character in regard to his own affairs receives a mocking comment from the tragedy that he provokes. In the "Amazing Marriage," the enormous pride and complex perverted psychology of a young lord are subjected to a shrewd light of ridicule by contrast with the natural simplicity of his plucky and devoted wife; and after long neglect, when he would assume the duties of a husband, he is denied the privilege. Thus the comic irony arises from a plot and a grouping of

persons carefully designed by the author to expose and set off the comic traits of character.
And in each case it involves an idea capable of
statement in words of wisdom if it is not sufficiently obvious on the face of the story.

I do not mean to make out the comic spirit
as a tyrant intolerant of anything romantic,
admirable, heroic. A comedy does not mean
with Meredith, any more than with Shakespeare,
a story in which all the characters are ridiculous.
For one egoist in Sir Willoughby, we have a
Clara, a Lætitia, a Vernon Whitford.   It is the
humorist and the satirist that offer a whole
gallery of originals. The comic artist puts on
the boards an actual group of human beings,
among whom the real and the unreal cast reflections on one another. Both parties gain by the
exchange. The complete natural simplicity of a
Sandra or a Carinthia is the best foil for the
fantastic excrescency of a Wilfrid or a Fleetwood.

Meredith's comedy is not even incompatible
with a tragic outcome for the stories. In the
case of the "tragic comedians," he undertakes
to show "how the comic in their nature led by
interplay to the tragic issue." Meredith does

not write tragedy. Tragedy celebrates the magnificence of heroic criminals, and the sunset splendors of star-crossed unfortunates. She chisels beauty out of the stern granite of fate. She is on the watch for grandeur. Comedy is content with less distinguished actors. Not crime but folly is her concern; and of fate she knows less than nothing. She does not flatter and exalt us with a sense of dusky mysteries and thrilling hazard. Her business is rather to prune the imagination, and with clarifying laughter restore the deluded to a right sense of values. But her laughter is not frivolous. She bids us reflect upon character as the maker of destiny; and sometimes from a wee rift in the lute she draws formidable and admonishing discords.

We must not suppose that Meredith put forward the comic as a special type of novel, offering the word as a label for the critic's application, like realist and romantic; that he wished to establish a new school of fiction, and compel all men to write comedy. "Life, we know too well," he says, "is not a Comedy, but something strangely mixed." He did not intend, himself, the writing of works that might be labelled comedy to the exclusion of romantic elements. He repudiates neither realism nor romance.[1] Romance is the quality that gives lift and inspiration. It is the chiming of overtones with the single note struck by the musician. If we let romance go, "we exchange a sky for a ceiling." Even a credible realism cannot be had without an element of the romantic; it would be to leave out human nature. But neither romance nor realism can dispense with the critical spirit of comedy.

Comedy Meredith proposed as a corrective, a disinfectant, a leaven. In launching his masterpiece, he indicates the two extremes of naturalism and sentimentalism as in need of comic discipline. Here he deplores in particular the dull prolixity of that philistine, "the realistic method of a conscientious transcription of all the visible, and a repetition of all the audible." Art is the specific he recommends for the disease of sameness; and he has in mind the art of the comic writer. What the naturalist lacks is not so much a sense of decency as a sense of humor.

In "Sandra Belloni" and the "Amazing Marriage," the analytic Philosopher, who represents the comic spirit, finds himself in a contest with

[1] For remarks on this subject, see "Amazing Marriage," XX, XXXIV, XXXVIII.

the old-fashioned romantic story-teller who wants
to get on with the story and cut out all impertinent questioning of motives. The Philosopher
wishes to analyze the motives of the Earl of
Fleetwood and lay bare the spring of his perverse
actions. "Dame Gossip prefers to ejaculate,
Young men are mysteries! and bowl us onward.
No one ever did comprehend the Earl of Fleetwood, she says." These are the cajoleries of
sentimentalism, the wilful blindness of a lazy
mind. These are the delusions that make men
ludicrous if not vicious. Lord Fleetwood has
the same easy way of disposing of his motives.
He does not himself understand why he wants
to do a certain mean thing. "He spied into
himself, and set it down to one of the many
mysteries. Men uninstructed in the analysis of
motives," says the Philosopher, "arrive at this
dangerous conclusion, which spares their pride
and caresses their indolence, while it flatters the
sense of internal vastness, and invites to head-
long intoxication." The Philosopher—or the
author—refuses to be a party to this comfortable
shifting of responsibility, to this sentimental self-
deception.

In "Diana," both offensive views of life are
passed in scornful review. The author of the

"Young Minister of State" is at one time sore tempted by the cheap triumphs of naturalism. "The world," she perceived, "imagines those to be at our nature's depths who are impudent enough to expose its muddy shallows." This view of things does not long hold Meredith's attention. At the other extreme is the sentimental view, so much more seductive, as it is an imitation of the spiritual. But "Philosophy bids us see that we are not so pretty as rose-pink, not so repulsive as dirty drab; and that instead of everlastingly shifting those barren aspects the sight of ourselves is wholesome, bearable, fructifying, finally a delight." This Philosophy is at one with the comic spirit in its intolerance of the spurious. "And how may you know that you have reached Philosophy? You touch her skirts when you share her hatred of the sham decent, her derision of sentimentalism." This is very like that Comedy that "watches over sentimentalism with a birch rod."

The comic spirit, then, is foe alike to the sentimental and the naturalistic style in fiction. The one is too fastidious to touch the material fact; the other will touch nothing else. There is in both cases a divorce of body and soul. Neither has robust imagination. Diana Merion was

advertised by her creator as a real woman, flesh
and spirit. The sentimentalist will acknowledge
no flaw in the spiritual beauty of his heroine;
the naturalist will scarce acknowledge the beauty,
he is so preoccupied with the flaw. Diana is,
the author boasts, "real flesh; a soul born active,
wind-beaten but ascending." She is not the
"true heroine of romance" because she is not
presented in that uncritical manner so flattering
to the humanity she represents. But to the
philosophic eye, she is an object of greater beauty;
for the philosopher loves nature "with the stem,
the thorns, the roots, and the fat bedding of
roses."

Diana is not a comic character, because she
does not make false pretensions to nobility. In
"Sandra Belloni" and the "Amazing Marriage,"
the "timid intrusions" of Philosophy are made
for the elucidation of characters actually comic,
because self-deceived. Without so much fuss,
Meredith has managed in other novels to subject
the characters to the same test. The Philosopher
and the Comic Spirit are not introduced in person; the indication of falsity is made, without
any flourish, in the mere statement of the character's acts, speech and reflections. But the
effect is the same. The comic essence closes

round and proves each character, dissolving what
is soft in each, but leaving in beautiful entirety
such as are entire. The result is far from merely
laugh-compelling; far likewise from the depress-
ing effect of merely negative criticism. There is
entertainment and edification to be had from the
exhibition of folly. Edifying and inspiring is the
portrayal of fair and noble character.

It is clear the laugh is an incidental consideration in Meredith's comedy. His aim is to make
us think. As we proceed in our study, we shall
realize more clearly the relation of Meredith's
comic method to his serious aims. Meredith's
art is not to be considered apart from his views
of life, like that of a mere story-teller. Nor
should his fiction be considered without reference
to his verse. In all his writing there appears a
distinct and harmonious *Weltanschauung*. Though
our present concern is with an aspect of his art,
we cannot fail to make some acquaintance with
his philosophy.

CHAPTER II

MEREDITH's first story is not comic; but it gives promise of comedy to follow. The "Shaving of Shagpat" is accurately described on the title-page as an Arabian Entertainment. It is a highly fanciful narrative of impossible adventures, in which a large part is played by magic.

The "Shaving of Shagpat" is a work of the imagination. Certain distinguished critics have been content to accept it as such, and to prize it for the fantastic charm of its inventions.[1] But there can be little doubt that parts at least have allegorical significance.[2] This is clear enough

---

[1] For example, Edmund Gosse in "Gossip in a Library," London, 1892, essay on the "Shaving of Shagpat"; George Eliot, articles in the "Leader," and the "Westminster Review" (see "George Meredith: Some Early Appreciations," by Maurice Buxton Forman. Scribner, 1909).

[2] We know the author was irritated with some bungling attempt to interpret the story, and that in the preface to the second edition he seems to repudiate the allegory. See Mr. Lane's bibliography (in Richard Le Gallienne's "George Meredith," etc., John Lane, 1905), page xv. But we know also that later he permitted the dedication to himself of an essay by a Scottish clergyman in which the

from the final chapter. We have been told the
exploits of Shibli Bagarag, the intrepid barber,
who succeeded in shaving the head of the clothier
Shagpat, against all the laws and prejudices of
the eastern world. This achievement was made
possible by the sharp and magical Sword of
Aklis. And now we read:

"Surely Shibli Bagarag returned the Sword to
the Sons of Aklis, flashing it in the midnight air,
and they, with the others, did reverence to his
achievement. They were now released from the
toil of sharpening the Sword for a half-cycle of
years. . . . ; for the mastery of an Event lasteth
among men the space of one cycle of years, and
after that a fresh Illusion springeth to befool mankind, and the Seven must expend the concluding
half-cycle in preparing the edge of the Sword for
a new mastery."

Here it stands written clearly enough that the
clothier Shagpat, or the special virtuous hair on
his head, the "Identical," finally cut away by
the prowess of the hero, signifies some kind of
long-established Illusion. We need not be more
explicit. As one commentator advises: "Inter-

allegory is explained in considerable detail. This is James
McKechnie's "Meredith's Shaving of Shagpat," Greenock,
James McKelvic and Sons, second edition, 1906. Mr.
McKechnie has recently made over his study; and the new
book appears under the title, "Meredith's Allegory, The
Shaving of Shagpat," Hodder & Stoughton, 1910. Pre-
fixed to this volume is a commendatory letter of Mere-
dith's referring to the earlier interpretation.

pret as freely as you choose. Any established
evil, any baneful superstition, any tyranny of
lies is Shagpat. Every age breeds its own Shagpat, and needs its own Shibli Bagarag. When
Luther accomplished his Reformation, he shaved
the Shagpat of his day, and that was a mighty
shave." [1]

Most of the story of Shibli Bagarag is purely
romantic and poetical. But there is an occasional incursion of the spirit of fun. The scenes
actually connected with the shaving of Shagpat
are conducted with a rare fantastic blend of the
humorous and the poetical. Incomparable in
drollery is the account of the unsuccessful attempt of Baba Mustapha, the hero's loquacious
uncle, to achieve the notable feat. He has
drugged his Shagpat and plastered him with
lather; and is on the point of proving himself
the veritable hero. All that prevents him is so
contemptible a creature as a flea. The heroism
of Baba Mustapha was evidently not of a kind
to withstand the terrible power of trivial dis-
tractions.

He is finally caught in his impious attempt
upon the hairy idol, and taken for trial before
the king. Here we are shown the apotheosis of

[1] McKechnie, 1906, page 9.

hair. The kings of all the world arrive to do homage to Shagpat. By way of displaying the might of the clothier, and punishing the wicked barber, Baba Mustapha is prodded on to his task of shaving the hairy one. Three times he approaches the inanimate white object, and three times, by the power of the Identical, he is shot violently away to a great distance.

ᶠ "And now a great cry rose from the people, as it were a song of triumph, for the Identical stood up wrathfully from the head of Shagpat, burning in brilliance, blinding to look on, he sitting inanimate beneath it; and it waxed in size and pierced through the roof of the hall, and was a sight to the streets of the city; and the horsemen camped without the wall beheld it, and marvelled, and it was as a pillar of fire to the solitudes of the Desert afar, and the wild Arab and wandering Bedouins and caravans of pilgrimage. . . . So the Identical burned in the head of Shagpat, as in wrath, three nights and three days. . . . So was the triumph of Shagpat made manifest to men and the end of the world by the burning of the Identical three days and three nights."

Was ever more fertile imagination devoted to the purposes of ridicule? For the triumph of Shagpat was short-lived. He was just about to meet with ignominy. But like the French monarchy before the Revolution, he had never seemed so magnificent. We need not be so specific in our interpretation of Shagpat and the Identical as in the interpretation of Holmes's "One-hoss Shay." But surely we have in this grotesque fantasy a burlesque suggestion of that seeming glorification of moribund institutions just before their going to pieces. The conception is worthy of Teufelsdröckh.

There follows a chapter in which the ludicrous passes into the phantasmagoric. The hero himself arrives, seated upon a great hawk, and in his hands the flashing Sword of Aklis. He is followed by his enemy Rabesqrat, Mistress of Illusions, streaming in the sky like a red disastrous comet. She seizes upon Shagpat, and carries him off like a doll, deep into the bowels of the earth. The battle of Rabesqrat and Shibli Bagarag has all the wild changes of the combats of genii in the Arabian Nights. Meantime one does not forget in the excitement the unheroic task in which the hero is actually engaged. And the narrative of the combat closes in the grave mock-heroic vein: "Day was on the baldness of Shagpat."

Take the work, if you choose, for mere extravaganza. Yet the theme cannot fail to prove suggestive in the light of the novels to follow. Nearly every one of them is devoted more or less to the exploding of illusions.   Such is the function of comedy.[1]   Such was the undertaking of Shibli Bagarag.   Meredith seems to foreshadow in this whimsical way what was to be the main business of his career.   The humorous symbolism of this Arabian tale is a fanciful counterpart to the realistic comedy of the novels.

No one can doubt that Meredith is a serious writer; that he has at heart the cause of human progress; that his aim is to contribute to that cause.   In a private letter, he says of his novels: "I think that the right use of life and the one secret of life is to pave the ways for the firmer footing of those who succeed us. . . . Close knowledge of our fellows, discernment of the laws of existence, these lead to great civilization. I have supposed that the novel exposing and illustrating the history of man may help us to such sustaining roadside gifts." [2]

Meredith has, it appears, the spirit of a reformer.   But he has not the gravity of many reformers.   And if his first published story is an

[1] Mr. Shaw, in a review of Meredith's "Essay," defines comedy as the "fine art of disillusion."   "For after all," he says, "the function of comedy . . . is nothing less than the destruction of old-established morals."   "Saturday Review," Mar. 27, 1897.

[2] I quote this from an article on "George Meredith and the World's Advance," by G. W. Harris in the "Independent," Feb. 13, 1908.

allegory of the battle for reform, neither he nor
his hero can dispense with a sense of humor.   A
sense of humor is what saves Shibli Bagarag from
the consequences of his own folly.   In the Palace
of Aklis, when he allows himself to be crowned
by the young beauties there, he is in danger of
losing his Mastery.   "Then they took the crown
and crowned him with it; and he sat upon the
throne calmly, serenely, like a Sultan of the great
race accustomed to sovereignty, tempering the
awfulness of his brows with benignant glances."
The reformer almost succumbs to the very fatuous vanity he is fighting.   And lo! he finds himself a prisoner, the ninety and ninth of those who
have vainly sought the Sword of Aklis.   Anguish
of self-condemnation releases him from confine-
ment with the other ninety-eight, but still he is
fixed to his foolish throne.   He longs for a drop
of the truth-telling waters of Paravid.   "So, as
he considered how to get at them from the seat of
his throne, his gaze fell on a mirror, and he beheld the crown of bejewelled asses' ears stiffened
upright, and skulls of monkeys grinning with
gems!   The sight of that crowning his head con-
vulsed Shibli Bagarag with laughter, and, as he
laughed, his seat upon the throne was loosened,
and he pitched from it."

The liberating power of laughter was strong in the mind of the author of Shagpat.[1] Earlier in the story we learn of the enchantress Goorelka and her aviary. Her birds are really men bewitched and denied the privilege of laughter. And we have a most exhilarating scene in which the rival enchantress Noorna sets them laughing over a story of men, and keeps them laughing an hour, till at last they are delivered.

Now the enchantress Noorna is Meredith, who sets us laughing over stories of men, and keeps us laughing until we are delivered from enchantment. Meredith is Shibli Bagarag wielding the Sword of Aklis.

This sword of wondrous properties, lengthened or shortened at will, making transparent whatever empty thing it is flashed upon, capable even of separating the thoughts in one's head, what should it be but the Sword of Common Sense celebrated later in the "Ode to the Comic Spirit"? The Sword of Common Sense was, like the Sword of Aklis,

"A lightning o'er the half-illumed,
Who to base brute-dominion cleave."

[1] For the clarifying virtues of laughter, compare the "Appeasement of Demeter"; passages in "A Faith on Trial," the "Empty Purse"; "Richard Feverel," XV; "Sandra Belloni," XXII; etc., etc.

The main business of the two swords is the same:

> ——"thou darest probe
> Old Institutions and Establishments,
> Once fortresses against the flood of sin,
> For what their worth.

*   *   *   *   *

> " Beneficently wilt thou clip
> All oversteppings of the plumed,
> The puffed, and bid the masker strip,
> And into the crowned windbag thrust,
> Tearing the mortal from the vital thing."

I do not wish to disturb those who find the "Shaving of Shagpat" an entertainment all-sufficing without reference to its symbolism. For myself, I find it most interesting as a poetic statement of Meredith's programme. Whether so intended or not, is of little consequence. Shibli Bagarag is for me a type of the comic artist puncturing illusions with the Sword of Common Sense.

CHAPTER III

THE WISEACRE

THE text of "Richard Feverel" has undergone
extensive revision since the first appearance of
the book in 1859.[1] The present version makes
a very different impression from that of the first
edition, largely owing to the difference in the
introductory chapters. In the original version,
it is not till the fifth chapter that we get started
on Richard's rick-burning escapade; and the
first four chapters are taken up chiefly with a
comic portrayal of Sir Austin and with droll il-

[1] There were two distinct revisions of "Richard Feverel," as pointed out by Hugh Chisholm in the "Acad-
emy," June 3, 1905. The first revised form appears in the
second edition in a single volume, Kegan Paul, 1878, and
in the Chapman and Hall editions of 1885, etc. The second revision, in which were made still further excisions,
was for the Constable edition of 1897. Our American editions from Scribner represent this ultimate form. We are
promised, in the last volume of the Memorial edition of
Meredith, a full account of the excisions and changes made
by Meredith in all his books. I have not personally con-
sulted the first revised form; but according to Mr. Chisholm's account, the great bulk of the material omitted in
the latest form was already cut out in the first revision.
The original three-volume edition of 1859 I have been able
to consult through the kindness of my friend Mr. William
E. Comfort of Des Moines.

lustration of the early workings of the System. Of other passages omitted in revision—including one long chapter in the second volume of the original—the bulk have to do with Sir Austin and his System, which are invariably treated in a gay spirit of ridicule. The result is that, while in its present form the story gives the impression of being the tragic history of Richard, in its original form it has more the effect of being the comic history of Sir Austin's System.

This is significant in relation to our theme. It seems clear that Meredith designed, in this first one of his novels, a comedy somewhat like that of Sir Willoughby Patterne; but that his prentice hand was not yet firm, the comic survey was not certain and consistent, and the uncertainty appeared in the product. Or, say, the design held within itself germs that were destined to shoot beyond it; the author was diverted from the comic point of view by the stirring and pathetic interest of his story. Tristram Shandy never emerged from the paternal and avuncular background to live a tragic life of his own and quicken the heartbeats of his readers. But Richard Feverel grew rapidly into an active and engaging hero little amenable to the purposes of comedy.

It is safe to say that this novel is highly prized for the tragedy of Richard and Lucy, and not for the comedy of Sir Austin.   And if his creature grew beyond his control, the author had grace enough to acknowledge him.   In preparing a second edition of the book, he realized that the story of Richard Feverel was too much delayed by the introductory bows of Sir Austin.   And he cut them short.   The Court of Ladies gathered at Raynham for the pursuit of the Griffin, though delicious creations after the recipe of Meredith's father-in-law, Peacock, were felt to be below the dignity of the muse of "thoughtful laughter," and especially out of place in a story so profoundly human as this.   The same judgment was later passed on the Dickens-upon-Fielding of Mrs. Caroline Grandison; and the chapter in which she appears was omitted in the second revision of 1897.

One cannot but admire the judgment of Meredith in his omissions.   In this self-denial, he perhaps sufficiently answers the complaint of Mr. Symons that English novelists cannot forbear the excessive use of humor.[1]   As a result of this condensation, the novel comes much nearer being

[1] See his "Note on George Meredith" in the "Fortnightly Review," Nov., 1897.

a consistent work of art. But the story has
sometimes suffered in point of clearness by
these omissions. Moreover, the parts omitted are very amusing; and in our study of
Meredith's comic method, and in relation to
his prevailing aims, they are of great interest.
In my account of Sir Austin, I shall make
reference largely to the material left out in
revision.

The system applied to Richard is an outcome
of Sir Austin's view of women as the source of
corruption, the chief menace to character; and
in the original version, the author sounds much
more loudly than in revision the note of ridicule
upon this theme. The first chapter records the
invasion of Raynham Abbey by a pack of women
bent on catching and converting the author of
the "Pilgrim's Scrip." The Baronet pretended
displeasure at the importunities of his Court, but
he was really much flattered by them. He was
compelled to acknowledge some virtue in a sex
that could appreciate his aphorisms. He is described as melting to woman, and indeed put into
very undignified comparison with St. Anthony.
Sir Austin was by no means wanting in suscep-
tibility to feminine charm. He was shown by
his published opinions of women to be a "senti-

mentalist jilted." "He was not splenetic: nay, he proved in the offending volume he could be civil, courteous, chivalrous, towards them: yet, by reason of a twist in his mental perceptions, it was clear that he looked on them as Domesticated Wild Cats." This is the point of view of that poet who wrote indulgently, "Thou art not false, but thou art fickle," and who had as great vogue with the sex he lampooned as the author of the "Pilgrim's Scrip." Sir Austin's views of women were very similar to those of the low-minded and cynical Adrian Harley. His attitude towards Austin Wentworth's marriage was the same as that of Sir Willoughby towards Vernon Whitford's. He could not appreciate the nobleness that could repair a moral offence with a *mésalliance*. It is not without significance that the good Sir Austin should have chosen the worldling for his favorite and turned away the imprudent but high-minded man. Worldly prudence he made the guardian of his hopes, rather than noble rectitude. It is an oblique comment on his System.

Sir Austin cannot forget the part played by woman in the fall of man; and the instinct of sex he names, accordingly, with obscure logic, the Apple-Disease, in allusion to the temptation in

the Garden.[1] His System is chiefly concerned
with protecting his son against the approaches of
this malady; and it has to receive humorous
reflections, in the first version, from the views of
the Court of Ladies. Mrs. M'Murphy, who is

[1] The invention of this Apple-Disease and of the Great
Shaddock Dogma seems to be one of those frolics of the
mystifying humorist such as Swift and Carlyle delighted
in. The Apple-Disease is sin, "an alien element in our
blood . . . with which Nature has striven since
Adam." (P. 18 of the 1859 ed. Compare also p. 20 for the
reference to the tree of Eden.) In the mind of Sir Austin,
the Apple-Disease and sin are always associated with the
temptations of sex. "You know my opinion, Doctor: we
are pretty secure from the Serpent till Eve sides with him."
But the Doctor "could not help thinking there were other
temptations than that one of Eve." (P. 70. Compare
also the second paragraph in Chapter XXXVII of the
present form.) An allusion to the Apple-Disease is made
by Adrian when he calls the period of Simple Boyhood the
Ante-Pomona stage (p. 62 of 1859). There remain allusions to this Apple-Disease in the present version. Most
significant is that in chap. XX, where we read that Richard
"had somehow learnt there was another half to the divided
Apple of Creation, and had embarked upon the great voy-
age of discovery of the difference between the two halves."
Compare also the chapter-head of XXIII and a passage
within the chapter.
    Sir Austin's views of women and of the temptations of
sex are embodied in the Great Shaddock Dogma. "So, on
account of its constant and ungenerous citation of the
primal slip in Paradise, Adrian chose to entitle 'The Pilgrim's Scrip'" (p. 7 of 1859). The several references to the
Great Shaddock Dogma in the original edition are helpful
in explaining the one enigmatic reference to it in the revised forms. At the end of chap. XXXIII of the ultimate
form (XXXIX of the first revision; chap. II of vol. III of
1859), we read of how Benson, the butler, was discharged
for having witnessed a sentimental passage between Sir
Austin and Lady Blandish, and "Raynham was quit of its
one believer in the Great Shaddock Dogma." This punish-
ment was the more unjust as Benson's intrusion had been

given some of the homely insight into human
nature later so illustrious in Mrs. Berry, has no
patience with the System. She "plainly told
Sir Austin, that, now young men had got the
taste for Apples, they would bite at them."
Accordingly the ladies gave up Sir Austin, and
"the System was left with a few occasionally-
visiting old Maids, eccentric wives, and the
neighbouring fair Widow Blandish, to work itself out, and then was peace again at Raynham
Abbey."

Mrs. Caroline Grandison makes her appear-

made in accordance with his faith in that dogma, in the
discharge of his function as guardian of Sir Austin against
the serpent-like wiles of woman. Benson had himself suffered a connubial misfortune. We read in the original edition, chap. IV, p. 60, "Benson was the 'Great Shaddock
Dogma' condensed in a look: potential with silence:—a
taciturn hater of Woman; burly, flabby, and implacable.
In him Sir Austin had his only faithful believer, and Adrian
his solitary rival. When, after 'The Pilgrim's Scrip' was
published, the fair ladies, its admirers, swarmed down to
form a court at Raynham, they were soon taught to stand
in fear of Heavy Benson, who read their object, and, if one
by chance got closeted with the Baronet, as they were all
seeking to do, a knock was sure to come, and Heavy Benson obtruded his glum person into the room on pressing
business, and would not go till he had rescued the prey."
Etc. There is another reference to the Great Shaddock
Dogma on p. 21 of the original edition.

My understanding of the Great Shaddock Dogma is
something like this. Shaddock is another name for grape-
fruit, which is by some taken to be the apple of Eden,
source of all our depravity. Now woman tempted man to
eat of the apple. Woman remains our chief tempter, the
root of sin. She is indeed the present apple of our temptation. She is the germ of the Apple-Disease.

ance later in a chapter of hilarious burlesque
entitled "A Shadowy View of Cœlebs Pater
going about with a Glass Slipper."[1] The amusing
employment of the Cinderella story for casting
ridicule upon the System harks back to the manner of "Shagpat." Frightened by symptoms of
Apple-Disease, Sir Austin has determined "that
not an hour must be lost in betrothing Richard,
and holding him bond to virtue." And behold
the father in the wicked metropolis seeking a
"mate worthy of the pure-blooded barb"! Mrs.
Caroline Grandison comes upon the rumor of
him everywhere.

"And an extremely unfavourable rumour it was,
for mothers who had daughters, and hopes for
their daughters, which a few questions of his had
kindled, and a discovery of his severe requisitions
extinguished. It appeared that he had seen nu-
merous young ladies. He had politely asked them
to sit down and take off their shoes; but such
monstrous feet they had mostly, that he declined
to attempt to try on the Glass Slipper, and politely
departed; or tried it on, and with a resigned sad
look declared that it would not, would not
fit! . . . .
"Some of the young ladies had been to schools.
Their feet were all enormously too big, and there

[1] This chapter stands between the chapters entitled "The
System Encounters the Wild Oats Special Plea" and "A
diversion played on a penny-whistle." The allusion in the
title is to Hannah More's edifying story of "Cœlebs in
Search of a Wife."

was no need for them to take off their shoes.
Some had been very properly educated at home;
and to such, if Bairam, physician, and Thompson,
lawyer, did not protest, the Slipper was applied;
but by occult arts of its own it seemed to find
out that their habits were somehow bad, and
incapacitated them from espousing the Fairy
Prince. The Slipper would not fit at all.

"Unsuspecting damsels were asked, at what
time they rose in the morning; and would reply,
at any hour. Some said, they finished in the
morning the Romance they had relinquished to
sleep overnight; little considering how such a
practice made the feet swell. Selina Rectangle
thought it a fine thing to tell him, she took
Metastasio to bed with her and pencilled trans-
lations of him when she awoke."

Then suddenly the author turns from the
System to the live human beings destined to mine
and blow it up. And the dramatic irony is
underscored in the glaring contrast.

"There was a damsel closer home, who did not
take Metastasio to bed with her, and who ate
dewberries early in the morning, whose foot, had
Sir Austin but known it, would have fitted into
the intractable Slipper as easily and neatly as
if it had been a soft kid glove made to her measure. Alas! the envious Sisters were keeping poor
Cinderella out of sight. Dewberries still abounded
by the banks of the river; and thither she strolled,
and there daily she was met by one who had the
test of her merits in his bosom; and there, on the
night the Scientific humanist conceived he had
alighted on the identical house that held the foot

to fit the Slipper, there, under consulting stars,
holy for ever more henceforth, the Fairy Prince,
trembling and with tears, has taken from her
lips the first ripe fruit of love, and pledged himself hers.

"A night of happy augury to Father and Son.
They were looking out for the same thing; only
one employed Science, the other Instinct; and
which hit upon the right it was for Time to decide.
Sir Austin dined with Mrs. Caroline Grandison."

Mrs. Caroline Grandison is to the great Sir
Charles what Joseph Andrews was to Pamela.
A lineal descendant of his, "in her sweet youth
this lady fell violently in love with the great Sir
Charles, and married him in fancy." On growing up, she would not relinquish his sacred name,
"and a quite unobjectionable gentleman was
discovered who, for the honour of assisting her
in her Mission, agreed to disembody himself in
her great name, and be lost in the blaze of Sir
Charles. With his concurrence, she rapidly produced eight daughters." All efforts failed to
realize "her saintly dream to have a Charles,"
and she had to be content with Charlotte and
Carola. But at last she heard of Sir Austin.
"All that was told her of the Baronet conspired
to make her believe he was Sir Charles in person
fallen upon evil times: the spirit of Sir Charles
revived to mix his blood with hers and produce

a race of moral Paladins after Sir Charles's pattern."

Mrs. Grandison had also a system. Her daughters must not be married "till she could find for them something like Sir Charles." Meantime she dosed them with medicine to keep their spirits low, and gave them daily exercise in the gymnasium to raise their bodily strength. Mrs. Grandison is clearly introduced as a companion piece to Sir Austin; and I need not be thought too fanciful in finding in her medicinal doses for her daughters a kind of symbolic counterpart to Sir Austin's own methods in the repression of Richard. A panegyric is hardly implied in the statement that "no lady living was better fitted to appreciate Sir Austin, and understand his System, than Mrs. Caroline Grandison."

The success of Mrs. Grandison in taking in Sir Austin is really too farcical for the serious art that prevails in this book. It would make of Sir Austin not a figure of high comedy, but one of those marionettes with which we are entertained in "Pickwick Papers." Unquestionably, Meredith made a wise sacrifice in cutting out this delicious chapter. But it is not the less significant for the light it throws on the original conception.

Still more significant are the passages, omitted
since 1878, in which is explained the meaning of
the title. The third chapter records a series of
petty tyrannies practised upon Richard as the
result of a superstitious fear especially ridiculous
in one who pretends to base his System on Science.
In the previous chapter, we have learned of a
sort of ancestral curse with which the house of
Feverel was dignified. "There was," the author
says, "a Mrs. Malediction in the house (be-
queathed by the great Sir Pylcher). Often had
she all but cut them off from their old friend,
Time, and they revived again. Whether it was
the Apple-Disease, or any other, strong con-
stitutions seemed struggling in them with some
peculiar malady." In other words, the ravages
of nature, commonly attributed to ill-luck, are
attributed in this distinguished family to a special
malice of the ruling powers. Sir Austin did not
at first succumb to this superstition.

"He had regarded his father, Sir Caradoc, as
scarce better than a madman when he spoke of a
special Ordeal for their race. . . . He was no
sooner struck hard than Sir Caradoc's words
smote him like a revelation. He believed that a
curse was in his blood; a poison of Retribution,
which no life of purity could expel; and grew,
perhaps, more morbidly credulous on this point
than his predecessor: speaking of the Ordeal of

the Feverels, with sonorous solemnity, as a thing incontrovertibly foredecreed to them." [1]

The Feverels, then, were in each generation destined to an Ordeal, which was not so much a trial of character as a menace of fate, a Scylla-Charybdis passage to be weathered. It was a malicious disease that threatened to wither the race by attacking the blossoms. These passages are of the greatest significance for the title of the book and the general design. The Apple-Disease that attacked so violently the subject of Sir Austin's Experiment is but the form of Ordeal to which Richard was destined as the inheritor of the family Malediction. This belief in a fore-decreed trial for his heir goes far to explain the perverse inaction of Sir Austin through the critical time when he actually held in his own hand the threads of destiny. Under the light of these passages, the Ordeal of Richard Feverel takes on a very different meaning from that naturally put

---

[1] A third time in this chapter the capitalized Ordeal of the Feverels is mentioned in a passage omitted in revision. Sir Austin's Ordeal was the unfaithfulness of his wife, the motherless state of his infant. The unlucky maid who cried out in sympathy for him on that midnight visit to his son, and joined her tears with his, must be discharged, we are told, because "to express sympathy for a Feverel during his Ordeal, was a grave misdemeanour." The word Ordeal is used apparently in this same meaning in the passages common to the original and the revised versions in XII and XXXIII of the present revised.

upon it. It is not primarily Meredith who applies the word to his hero, but Sir Austin. In the mouth of the author, it is a mock at the pseudo-scientific Baronet.

The reader of Meredith knows how scornful he is of the inclination to throw on fate the responsibility for the course of one's life. This sort of superstition is a great foe to happiness and progress. It leads one to neglect a study of the real causes, outside or within one's self, that lead to disaster or success. It is natural among ignorant people and excusable in those who do not pretend to a knowledge of nature. But for a man to devise a *scientific* system for avoiding *destiny* is an absurd paradox. It is, however, a familiar one; and Sir Austin is here a type of bewildered humanity. Viewed in this light, the story takes on a large representative character, half comic, half pathetic.

Of course, the ordeal, or risk, which takes on this comic hue from the superstition of the Baronet is to be regarded seriously also as a trial of character for the young man, an ordeal of refining fire. Perhaps this is the conception most prominent in the reader's mind. And indeed the Baronet himself seems so to consider the ordeal, over and above his notion of the peculiar destiny of the Feverels. Moreover, Lady Blandish and the thoughtful reader perceive this to be in reality the Ordeal of Sir Austin. He is on trial quite as much as his son. Thus, the word takes on a variety of meanings according to the angle from which it is viewed. It is always Meredith's joy to give an incident or phrase as many facets as possible for the reflection of varied complementary colors. There is a kind of wit in this,—a long-range play upon words, in which the several ideas connoted by the same word throw glancing lights back and forth upon one another.

Sir Austin has early confirmation of his superstitious faith. On the morning of his seventh birthday, the Hope of Raynham relates a vision of a lady who visited him in the night. Sir Austin at once scents Mrs. Malediction. We are assured at the end of the chapter that it was actually the boy's wretched mother that appeared to him. But Richard's account of the "dream," much enlarged upon with childish eloquence, so greatly alarms the Baronet that every harmless amusement is denied his son lest the omen prove genuine. The Baronet will not admit that he does "perhaps altogether believe in supernatural visitations." But "call it what you will. It is in the habit of coming to us when something is about to happen." Consequently the seven-year-old is jealously guarded from water and from fire, from the perils of riding and eating. And—supreme humiliation—he is ordered to strip for medical examination.

We have here a miniature map of the system of surveillance and repression: here and throughout, it is dictated by superstition; and the present explosion foreshadows the more tragic one that follows. Richard refused to go to the Doctor.

This preliminary Ordeal of Richard turned out to be that of his uncle Algernon. Richard returned from the examination—for "of course he had to go"—in time to witness the "Catastrophe of the day." Uncle Algernon, he of the beautiful legs, lost one of them in a cricket match.

" 'Said I not, Something would happen?' remarked Sir Austin, not altogether dissatisfied.

" 'Oh, confound Mrs. Malediction!' Algernon groaned to Colonel Wentworth.

" 'You're as staunch a believer in her now as Austin,' said the Colonel." [1]

It is understood that Uncle Algernon is the scapegoat, and has received the anticipated blow

[1] This is from chap. III in 1859, entitled "Mrs. Malediction." The superstition of Sir Austin is still further illustrated in chap. V, "Showing how the fates selected the fourteenth birthday to try the strength of the System." There we learn of a sympathetic cypress tree, whose shadow dogs the steps of a Feverel doomed to an Ordeal.

of Mrs. Malediction, has experienced one of the
Ordeals of the Feverels.

The actual Ordeal of Richard comes after his
marriage. And here it becomes clear that this
constitutes the Ordeal of Sir Austin. Here we
see the Baronet "on trial under the eyes of the
lady who loved him." The news of his son's
marriage was a terrible blow to his pride both as
Theorist and head of a Family. But instead of
the natural expression of his feelings, he summoned all his powers to the simulation of that
philosophic calmness so essential to his character
as the author of a System. And so he sat "nurs-
ing the devil," while he supposed himself to be
conducting the Ordeal of his son. Equally
distant from a reasoned science and a natural
humaneness, he masked his wounded feelings
under the pretence of giving his son a trial. And
up to the last he maintained his fatuous dignity
and assumption of scientific infallibility, unmoved
by the tragic spectacle of what he had brought
about. Lady Blandish had read him through
before the end; and her concluding letter to
Austin Wentworth contains her verdict on his
tragi-comic performance.

One will hardly get satisfaction from an attempt
to show how the story of Richard Feverel con-

demns the system of Sir Austin. The marriage
with Lucy was not a mistake, however much it
may have seemed so, and it cannot be laid to a
vicious system of education.[1] The affair of Mrs.
Mount, and all the tragedy, was provoked by the
senseless separation of Richard from his wife,
which is perhaps to be traced to Sir Austin's
pique rather than to his system.[2] I think
Meredith's intention was larger than this; that
what he wished to condemn was not so much a
particular system as the folly of putting faith in
any rigid system, folly that would offer any
system as a substitute for humane regard to the
individual. Sir Austin went so far as to pre-
scribe the age at which his son should marry, and
insist on postponing that event for more than
fifteen years. The boy was fourteen, and had
already shown signs of approaching manhood,
when his father informed Doctor Clifford he
should not be married till his thirtieth year.
"He need not marry at all," suggests the Doctor.
"On my System he must marry," rejoins the
inflexible Sir Austin.

[1] Except in its prematureness.
[2] Of course, we may say, the System made him more in-
nocently open to the seductions of Mrs. Mount,—more
Quixotic in his effort to serve her, and more susceptible to
her charms. But it is simple folly rather than the System
that kept him in London during the time of his Ordeal.

In the first edition we are given a synopsis of
Sir Austin's Note-book, "wherein the youth's
progressionary phases were mapped out in sec-
tions, from Simple Boyhood to the Blossoming
Season, the Magnetic Age, The Period of Pro-
bation, from which, successfully passed through,
he was to emerge into a Manhood worthy of
Paradise." The use of capital letters is interesting. It does not stop with the designation of
these periods. Everything related to the System,
everything related to Sir Austin's philosophy of
life, is accorded this burlesque dignity. To this
System, persons are not persons but types, abstractions proper for the use of the Aphorist.
Sir Austin is a Theorist with a large T. The
inductive method is as unfamiliar to him as to
the scholastic philosophers; and Meredith, living
in an age of experimental science, represents a
Scientific humanist whose practice is absurdly at
variance with his profession. When Mrs. Grandison was showing Sir Austin her girls' gymnasium,
he did not observe the girls themselves. "The
Baronet was too much wrapped up in the enlight-
enment of her principle, to notice the despondency
of their countenances." The aphoristic custom
of dealing with abstractions has become a habit;
and while eminently skilful in the handling of

Good and Evil, of Wisdom and Education, Man and Woman, Youth and Manhood, Sir Austin is blind and helpless in the actual presence of a particular boy or woman. Such incapacity is common enough, and not in itself comic. It is the complacent and undisputed assumption of Wisdom that makes so ridiculous the want of it.

Sir Austin Feverel was a rather foolish man who assumed an air of wisdom. He was a man of temperament far from scientific who laid claim to science. He was a bungler who thought himself expert. The bungler is not humorous merely as bungler; but he becomes so on the slightest pretence of dexterity. There is no claim more open to ridicule than the claim of science. We can more readily pass by an exaggerated estimate of one's physical beauty, of one's social importance, of one's moral strength. These all are included in Plato's definition of the ridiculous as rooted in self-ignorance. But these errors are the errors of allowedly ignorant men, who do not rest their plea for respect on the correctness of their knowledge and judgment. It is natural for them to be mistaken. But the scientist must of all things be right. He must command the facts. And when we find a man, notoriously in error, who prides himself above all on his infallibility, we are at the very fountain-head of the ludicrous.

Sir Austin was a practical scientist dealing in human nature; and the one thing he left out of account was human nature. His was an abstract theory formed in advance of experiment, that would yield no jot to the suggestions arising from experiment. For he did not engage in experiment for the sake of getting information, of determing the truth or falsehood of his theory. He assumed without question the truth of his theory; and his experiment was by way of testing the subject. He was merely applying litmus paper to this substance, to see whether it was basic or acid. He would have been wiser to test the worth of his litmus paper by the correctness of its report on the subject of experiment.

From the first Meredith shows himself a comic writer. But he does not show from the first the sureness in conception and execution of comic designs that marks his later work. His first novel may be characterized, from our point of view in this study, as a *comédie manquée*. In the first place, the comic idea is somewhat obscure. The figure of Sir Austin was never quite released from the block in which the artist sought him. But this is not all. There is a question of the prevalence of comic treatment. The comic idea becomes subordinate to the tragic interest of the story. In this chapter, we have had a double task. We have had, not only to expound the comic idea, but to show that the design *is* primarily comic. In relation to the comedies to follow, this obligation does not rest upon us: we may assume that the design is comic, and we have only to expound the comic idea.

"Richard Feverel" stands by itself among the comedies of Meredith. The Wiseacre, as such, is a solitary figure, not closely related to the other comic personages in Meredith's gallery. In the novels that follow, we find certain comic types recurring over and over again, types in various ways related to one another, and, taken all together, making up what we may regard as a progressive series. And the study of this series possesses, I think, a certain continuous philosophical interest. In the chapter on the Comic Philosophy, but not till then, shall we be able to view the first comic study in its relation to the whole series.

CHAPTER IV

BETWEEN "Richard Feverel" and the "Egoist" I count five distinctively comic stories: "Evan Harrington," "Sandra Belloni," "Harry Richmond," "The House on the Beach," "General Ople and Lady Camper." They fall in one group among Meredith's novels both chronologically and as to subject matter. I take the liberty of applying to them collectively a title made illustrious by Thackeray in the "Book of Snobs." For snobbery in one form or another is the prevailing theme of these stories.

A snob, I take it, is one who has for wealth and social distinction a regard out of proportion to their real value. If he is himself elevated in these respects, he is inclined to scorn those beneath him, and to assume a superiority not justified to the philosophic view. If he is down himself, he is frantic to get up, still more to seem up. Strictly, I understand, the word describes one who pretends to a social distinction not rightly his; but

56

the meaning of the word has been extended. Snobbery is most striking in the comfortable middle classes. The peasant is beneath hope and pretence. The noble can afford to be magnanimous. But the well-to-do citizen, with every want supplied save what springs from vanity, has for his chief business in life the cultivation of "society." "Having received a great deal of obloquy," says witty Thackeray, "for dragging monarchs, princes, and the respected nobility into the Snob category, I trust to please everybody . . . by stating my firm opinion that it is among the *respectable* classes of this vast and happy empire that the greatest profusion of Snobs is to be found."

Equally with his lighter sketches, the great novels of Thackeray have for their central aim the satiric delineation of snobbery. High snobbery we might call it in him; for Pendennis and Ethel Newcome and Becky Sharp move on an elevated plane. Low snobbery is a chief theme of Dickens, who celebrates the humble aspirations of Kenwigses, the lowly pride of Lillyvicks and Snevelliccis. Neither Dickens nor Thackeray has displayed so much ingenuity as Meredith in the conception of comic plots upon this theme; neither has approached him in fineness of insight, in thoughtfulness of treatment, above all in imagination. Both surpass him in simplicity of statement; and by consequence, they make a broader appeal, and may boast an element of good art somewhat wanting to Meredith.

The snob is not so complex a character as the sentimentalist or the refined egoist. The portrayal of snobbery does not require so great subtlety of analysis, so deep a sounding of the heart. Accordingly, we shall find little in the Book of Snobs that is specially distinctive of Meredith; and those who wish to come promptly at his peculiar and original contributions to comedy are recommended to pass over this chapter and proceed immediately to the one that follows. But the author cannot do so with a good conscience; for no discussion of Meredith's comic writing would be complete without some consideration of the well-known stories that make up his Book of Snobs.

Funniest of Meredith's snobs is General Ople. This middle-class gentleman is no hopeless victim of social ambition. His genteel affectations are superficial; and he fortunately encounters a lady of superior station and sterling sense to take the nonsense out of him. General Ople is not quite *au fait* socially. But he wishes to be thought so.

And he prides himself on the very phrases and
sentiments that give him away.   He is like the
Irishwoman in Maria Edgeworth who betrayed
her strangeness to London by too correct a London accent.   But his snobbery appears most
pronounced in relation to his daughter's marriage
to Lady Camper's nephew.   Lady Camper demands that he make over a good sum for his
daughter's provision.   Ten thousand pounds is
the sum she names.   Ten thousand pounds
would cripple the General, and leave him some
day at the mercy of his wife.   But he wishes to
be thought well-to-do.   He has not the courage
to confess to the smallness of his income.   He is
finally brought to this confession by the ingenious
persecutions of Lady Camper.   His snobbery,
together with his masculine vanity and egoism,
succumbs to the battery of ridicule she turns
upon him.

The "House on the Beach" offers an instance
of more radical snobbery in a figure conceived
with rare drollery of imagination.   Mart Tinman
would seem at first to belong rather to the reper-
tory of Smollett or Dickens than to that of Meredith.   Retired tradesman turned squire, but still
tradesman in all his ways, he reminds one of Mr.
Gamaliel Pickle.   Like Mr. Pickle, he has a

scheming and congenial sister concerned to marry
him to advantage. He has been rejected by
every marriageable woman of means in the neigh-
borhood. A most uninspiring personality; but
he has imagination all the same. He is actually
bailiff of the Cinque Port in which he lives; and
he looks forward to some occasion, not inconceivable, in which he may be presented at court
to read an address to majesty. In view of this
contingency, the illiterate man practises reading
aloud to his sister; and he spends long hours in
secret posing before a cheval glass in silken
small-clothes. He leads a rich and visionary life
behind the drawn curtains of his dulness.

When an old friend returns from Australia,
Mart Tinman receives him with cold caution till
he learns of his wealth, and then he sets out to
marry the rich man's daughter. He has a hold
on his friend through knowledge of a compro-
mising secret, and he tries to force the marriage
by threatening to disclose the secret. But the
two men don't get along very well; and when at
last his friend breaks the engagement, Mart
Tinman writes a letter of betrayal.

But the letter was never posted. Meantime,
the sea has risen, and a terrible storm threatens
Tinman's home, the House on the Beach. The

fatuous man is a long time oblivious of the danger, occupied with his royal romance. For hours, while the storm rages, he remains posing before the glass in his court dress. He has to be rescued by a party sent out by his friend Van Diemen. His property is all lost,—his land engulfed by the waves.

The conclusion is marked by the comic betrayal of his quaint ambitious dream. On being received by his friends on shore, Tinman is for a moment perched on the sea wall. "In this exposed situation, the wind, whose pranks are endless when it is once up, seized and blew Martin Tinman's dressing-gown wide as two violently flapping wings on each side of him, and finally over his head. Van Diemen turned a pair of stupefied flat eyes on Herbert, who cast a shy look at the ladies. Tinman had sprung down. But not before the world, in one tempestuous glimpse, had caught sight of the Court suit." Never was more strange, original and yet convincing embodiment of the aristocratic spirit.

General Ople has but a slight alloy of snobbery in a composition of amusing ingredients. Mart Tinman dwells in the obscure suburbs of snobbery; he is a rare and special type. These stories are both slight incidental sketches. In

"Evan Harrington," we have a large and serious canvas devoted to illustration of the world of snobs, and offering a number of varied types in persons acting out an ingenious comic plot. In good society itself we have displayed the scorn of those in a station below. There is the *parvenu,* zealous in covering the track by which he arrived. There is ridiculous pretence in the obviously vulgar. And most important of all, in considering the distinctive in Meredith, the hero himself is not always free from snobbery. His struggle to free himself from all scent of it constitutes what we may call his comic ordeal.

Evan Harrington is the son of a tailor, most ignominious of trades; but he has the fortune, or misfortune, to have been bred like a gentleman, and to possess the instincts and manners going with gentle birth. His sisters have all, by marriage, managed to rise above their class; and they conspire to raise their brother into good society by similar means. To this end they agree to rescue him from his father's trade, and to suppress all mention of the deceased father: procedure which, for the rest, they must necessarily follow for the maintenance of their own prestige.

Their father was in his day a snob. At least

he was more than once called so by no less an
authority than Lady Jocelyn. Melchisedec Harrington had achieved the miracle of being received for a gentleman in the countryside which
he served as a tailor. But if Lady Jocelyn calls
him "a snob, and an impostor," that is because
she is not fully acquainted with his history. He
had indeed, at one time, the ambition to pass, at
Bath, for more than he was, and he allowed himself to be thought a marquis in disguise. But
we are assured that afterwards he had the courage
and the good sense to shun all assumption. He
desired, as the tailor said himself, "to have his
exact measure taken everywhere." His double
life was not a dishonest one; and he was a paradox, not an impostor.

The "great Mel" is proclaimed to be dead at
the opening of the story; and he takes no part
in it except that of a ghost. But he proves a
ghost very hard to lay, as the Harringtons learn
to their discomfiture.

The central comic figure among the living is
Louisa Harrington. She has married a count,
albeit Portuguese and penniless, and she boasts
the high-sounding title of Countess de Saldar de
Sancorvo. Wonderful are the stories of high
life she brings from the Portuguese court; only,

it is suggested, they are the product of a snobbish imagination working over incidents from low life in an English town. The Countess de Saldar is leader in the conspiracy for burying the ghost of her father, and contriving the advantageous marriage of her brother. She is a great general, a field marshal. She displays the genius of a Becky Sharp. The great tests of generalship come when the Countess is established at Beckley Court, the home of Rose Jocelyn. She has with her, sister Caroline and brother Evan. Evan has nearly won the heart of the aristocratic young lady. But word is passed around among some of the young gentlemen that Evan Harrington is a tailor's son; and the Countess makes it her business to handle these young gentlemen. Meantime she is pleased to observe that Caroline, who has left her brute of a husband, finds favor with a real English duke. So aristocratic a connection decidedly strengthens the position of the tailor's children.

This comic victim is always provoking her own fate. The great scene in what we may call Act III of the comedy is one "in which the daughters of the great Mel have to digest him at dinner." There comes to Beckley Court a country squire who had once known the Harrington girls, had

indeed gone so far as to elope with Louisa. Squire
Uploft cannot think of identifying with his early
flame this magnificent noblewoman with a foreign
accent. But the dinner proves one fiery ordeal
for the two sisters. Squire Uploft has struck an
interesting theme in the exploits of the great
Mel. The Countess leads the conversation; but
whatever topic she starts, the talk returns to her
unhappy father. At last George Uploft relates
a story about the eldest daughter so painful to
Caroline that she faints away and breaks up the
feast with most admired disorder. Act IV in-
troduces situations equally embarrassing to the
children of the shears.

Innumerable were the sacrifices made by
Louisa Harrington for her ambition. Neither
she nor either of her sisters dared attend the
funeral of their father. She was obliged to tell
many lies, not the less real lies for their being
implicit. She had to resort to unworthy means
to win the good will of one young gentleman, and
to actual forgery for securing the banishment of
another hostile one. She must disregard morality
and decency in the encouragement of her sister's
liaison. She must suffer constantly the pangs of
discovery. And she gained nothing by it all in
the end. While she was bending every energy

to hoodwink the Jocelyns, Evan had revealed
the truth, and was about to reap the reward of
honesty. As it proved, the schemes of the
Countess were in the end what banished them
from Beckley. And the final success of Evan
was made in the teeth of her policy.

She was a thorough snob, far more of one than
any of the born gentlefolk. Hers was the extreme snobbishness of the *parvenu*. She could not
conceive that a tailor might be thought a gentleman. She would not like to conceive it. She
would maintain the barrier between trade and
gentility. What had she gained herself if all
tailor's daughters might become countesses? She
could not imagine native gentility, nobleness
apart from title. It is the essence of snobbishness to regard the rank instead of the
man.

In this the true gentlefolk showed a more open
mind and more capacity for instruction. At the
start Rose displayed the prejudice of her class.
She preferred "English gentleman" to "Englishman" as a designation for Evan; and when he
asked her to define the word "gentleman," she
replied, with fine dramatic irony in view of the
facts, "Can't tell you. . . . Something you
are, sir." But in the end, things were so

completely reversed that her only doubt was
not whether the tailor was a gentleman, but
whether a certain nobleman might prove to
be one.

Louisa Harrington is a broadly humorous
character. More distinctive of Meredith I find
the treatment of the hero himself. Infinitely
removed from the class of "humors," he is nevertheless at times a comic figure. And being the
hero, the one with whom the reader identifies
himself, we find in him a comic representation
of ourselves.

He is comic just in so far as he falls into the
dishonesty that makes so ridiculous his sister.
Every surrender to snobbery provokes the laughter of the wicked little imps. The reader will
remember those creatures that made game of the
Egoist,—how penetrating they were in the perception of the comic. It is interesting to observe
in "Evan Harrington" a much earlier appearance
of these sprites, trained already in the discovery
of subtle traits of humor. They set upon Evan,
we are told, just when he was determining to per-
form an heroic deed. "Malignly do they love
to uncover ridiculousness in imposing figures,"
says the author of the "Egoist."

Shall Evan prove a snob, an impostor? That

is the question that determines whether he shall
be abandoned to the imps.[1]

His most signal triumph over snobbery appears
in that festive scene at the Green Dragon, when
he was on his way to London to learn his father's
trade in order to pay his father's debts.   He had
with him a friend of his schooldays, picked up on
the road, a shabby fellow of theatrical propen-
sities, who would like to be thought a gentleman
and a scholar.   Evan was humiliated with the
foolish attempts of Raikes to impress the company with his aristocratic tastes, and was driven
himself to the opposite extreme of humility.

It will be remembered that Mr. Raikes, at this
supper party, having taken more ale than was
good for him, made a feeble attempt at oratory.
Certain young gentlemen present among the
farmers—certain actual gentlemen—showing a
disposition to make fun of him, a quarrel arose
that led to Evan's remarkable confession.

Having twice repeated the introductory "Gentlemen!" Jack was in peril of ignominious laughter.   But he recovered himself in the moment of
danger.

[1] A gently humorous treatment of the hero is pursued
in the earlier chapters "On board the Jocasta" and "My
gentleman on the road."

"With a dramatic visage, he leaned over his glass, and looking as he spoke from man to man, asked emphatically, 'Is there any person present whose conscience revolts against being involved in that denomination?'. . .

"Jack's readiness had thus rescued him in extremity.

"He nodded, and went ahead cheerily.

" 'I should be sorry to think so. When I said "Gentlemen," I include all. If the conscience of one *should* impeach him or me——' Jack eyed the lordly contemplator of his nails on a pause, adding, 'It is not so. I rejoice. I was about to observe, then, that, a stranger, I entered this hospitable establishment—I and my friend——'

" 'The gentleman!' their now recognized antagonist interposed, and turned his head to one of his comrades and kept it turned—a proceeding similar in tactics to striking and running away.

" 'I thank my honorable— a— um! I thank the— a— whatever he may be!' continued Jack. 'I accept his suggestion. My friend, the gentleman!— the real gentleman!— the true gentleman!— the undoubted gentleman!' " [1]

Still further remarks led to more stress on the word gentleman; but I stop with this emphatic labelling of Evan. We are reminded of the humorous sub-title of the novel in the original

---

[1] Some of the passages I quote from this scene have been cut out in the revised form of the story. I quote from the pirated Harpers ed. of 1860, which seems, as far as I have compared them, to be identical with the form as published in "Once A Week," Feb. to Oct., 1860. Meredith may have made some improvement in the frequent excisions in the later version. But in certain cases, the author's design appears more strikingly in the original.

form, "Evan Harrington, or, He would be a
Gentleman."

The two varieties of snobbery are set forth by
the author in an indication of the feelings of
the adversaries. "In that young gentleman he
[Raikes] had recognized one of a station above
his own . . . ; and he did not intend to
allow it. On the other hand Laxley had begun
to look at him very distantly over the lordly
bridge of his nose. To Mr. Raikes, Laxley was
a puppy: to Laxley, Mr. Raikes was a snob.
The antagonism, therefore, was natural: ale did
but put the match to the magazine."

Evan was neither puppy nor snob, and he took
no part in the wrangle. The gentlemen took him
for one of themselves who had picked up the low
fellow on a whim. But when he found himself
directly challenged to fight for his friend, he felt
bound to let it be known he was not a qualified
adversary. You may be sure that he would
rather have fought, that he was not wanting in
physical courage. He had been wincing under
the references of Raikes, at each repetition of the
word gentleman. "Tailordom bellowed in his
ears every fresh minute: 'Nothing assume.' "

"There was a disdainful smile on Evan's mouth
as he replied: 'I must enlighten you. I have

no pretensions to your blue blood or yellow.   If,
Sir, you will deign to challenge a man who is *not*
the son of a gentleman, and consider the expression of his thorough contempt for your conduct
sufficient to enable you to overlook that fact,
you may dispose of me.   My friend here has, it
seems, reason to be proud of his connections.
That you may not subsequently bring the charge
against me of having led you to "soil your
hands"—as your friend there terms it—I, with
all the willingness in the world to chastise you
or him for your impertinence, must—as I conceive I am bound to do—first give you a fair
chance to escape, by telling you that my father
was a tailor, and that I also am a tailor.' "[1]

Here we have a recurrence of the declaration
of the great Mel at Squire Uploft's dinner-table.
True son of his father, Evan left small opening
here for the shafts of the comic imps.

But alas! he was not always to behave with
such heroism.   Getting by accident a glimpse of
Rose, he allows himself to be carried off to Beckley
and to become subservient for a time to the dishonest policy of his sister.   Then comes the
mysterious letter from Tom Cogglesby, in which
he is offered a handsome competence if he will
agree to become a tailor.   The heads of two
succeeding chapters here display the most strik-

[1] The only difference between the two versions in this
speech is that the revised form leaves out the last seven
words.

ing moment of comedy in the career of Evan
Harrington. In Chapter XVII, "Evan writes
himself Tailor"; in XVIII, "Evan calls himself
Gentleman."

Never was the genius of dishonesty to make a
bigger fool of Evan than during the scene in
which he gave Laxley assurance that he was
qualified to fight him, and was admitted by the
latter into the ranks of gentlemen. Evan was
intending now to leave Beckley for good; but
was easily persuaded to remain on the pretext of
Caroline's need of him. He knew himself to be
managed, and gave up his will into the keeping
of another. He was far from heroic at this stage
of his career.

He received the first instalment of money supplied on condition of his becoming a tailor. But
he continued the game at Beckley. "Evan held
in his pocket the price of his bondage to Tailordom, while he was every instant sealing his assumption of the character of Gentleman." The
trouble with him was that he still accepted for
himself the false standards of others. "He was
of dull brain, and it had not yet dawned on him
that he might possibly be tailor and gentleman in
one." [1] He was not an adventurer plotting to

[1] Quoted from the original version, XXIV, which bears

entrap the unsuspecting damsel. It was not so
much his fear of losing Rose that prevented his
confession as his fear of losing her respect. Not
so much love as pride was bleeding in him.

At last he summoned courage to make confession, and at once received his reward. He found
Rose a staunch defender of him before the world.
She was now scornful of the conventional use of
the word gentleman. She had long since defined
gentleman to Evan as "something you are, sir."

Meantime we have neglected Jack Raikes.
What connection has this droll fellow with the
comic history? I confess that, as an individual
character, Jack Raikes seems to me a failure.
He has not that spontaneous and irresponsible
charm that characterizes his fellows in Dickens:
he cannot compare with Dick Swiveller for personal fascination. In the condensed version, he
has been cut so as to be hardly intelligible. He
is a clumsy, grotesque, bewildering person, always in the way.

I believe Jack Raikes was introduced as a sort
of burlesque shadow of Evan Harrington. As
we find the follies of gentlefolk more amusing in

the title "Chronicles the return of Mr. Raikes," and contains more matter than the corresponding chapter in the
revision, entitled "The Countess makes herself felt."

servants, those of white people in darkies, grown-
ups in children; so we may laugh at Evan in his
parody Jack. He is parody, and foil, and dreadful warning to the hero. Though Evan "would
be a gentleman," he has generally sense enough
to forbear assumption: Jack is not afraid to show
off his qualifications. It is Jack's insistence on
the title of gentleman that leads Evan to repudiate
that title for himself. But while Evan is persuaded to write himself tailor, he shortly after
declares himself gentleman. Jack Raikes envies
Evan's fortune, and boasts to Old Tom what a
gentleman *he* is. Tom offers to make him a man
of means and an M. P. if he will wear on his back
a tin plate inscribed "John F. Raikes, Gentleman." [1] Here the parody is obvious enough.
Again, Evan is in love with an heiress. Jack, in
his noon of fortune, conceives the most rosy
possibilities for himself in the matrimonial line.
Behold him in society.

"Mr. Raikes made his way toward a company he perceived on the lawn. His friend
Harrington chanced to be closeted with Sir
Franks: the Countess de Saldar was in her
chamber: no one was present whom he knew
but Miss Jocelyn, who welcomed him very cor-
dially, and with one glance of her eyes set the

[1] XXXII. This is made much more intelligible in the
original form.

mercurial youth thinking whether they ought to
come to explanations before or after dinner; and
of the advantages to be derived from a good
matrimonial connection, by a young member of
our Parliament. He soon let Miss Jocelyn see
that he had wit, affording her deep indications of
a poetic soul; and he as much as told her that,
though merry by nature, he was quite capable
of the melancholy fascinating to her sex, and
might shortly be seen under that aspect. He
got on remarkably well till Laxley joined them;
and then, despite an excessive condescension on
his part, the old Fallowfield sore was rubbed, and
in a brisk passage of arms between them, Mr.
John Raikes was compelled to be the victor—to
have the last word and the best, and to win the
laughter of Rose, which was as much to him as
a confession of love from that young lady. Then
Juliana came out, and Mr. Raikes made apologies
to her, rejecting her in the light of a spouse at the
first perusal of her face. Then issued forth the
swimming Countess de Saldar, and the mutual
courtesies between her and Mr. Raikes were
elaborate, prolonged, and smacking prodigiously
of Louis Quatorze. But Rose suffered laughter
to be seen struggling round her mouth; and the
Countess dismayed Mr. Raikes by telling him
he would be perfect by-and-by, and so dislocating
her fair self from the ridicule she opened to him—
a stroke which gave him sharp twinges of un-
easiness, and an immense respect for her. The
Countess subsequently withdrew him, and walked
him up and down, and taught him many new
things, and so affected him by her graces that
Mr. John Raikes had a passing attack of infidelity to the heiress." [1]

[1] This passage was cut out in revision.

Young Evan, towards the end, developed a
sense of humor in relation to himself; and he
came to see in Jack "something of himself magnified," a "burlesque of himself." Thus we perceive the significance of this broadly humorous
figure for the fine comic delineation of the hero.
The author spared Evan on the principle that "a
hero should be held as sacred as the Grand
Llama." The imps are held in leash, and not
allowed to make with him the havoc they made
with Sir Willoughby. Sir Willoughby was not
the hero, not the gentleman destined to carry off
the chosen lady. He is open to comic treatment
because we have a Vernon Whitford on whom the
reader may lavish his sympathetic concern. But
this hero is destined to win the golden girl; and
he must not be allowed to wander too far from
the straight road of honest heroism. And so, to
bear his comic burden, there is invented his
quaint fantastic friend, in whom, as in a convex
mirror, we behold a monstrous distorted image
of himself, or of what he so easily might have
been. In Evan we recognize in rudiment the
snobbish instincts common to us all; in Jack
Raikes and the Countess de Saldar, we see them
rank and full-blown, grotesque, ill-smelling weeds,

bearing in their absurd magnificence a ludicrous resemblance to ourselves.

In general pattern and purport, there is a close resemblance between "Evan Harrington" and "Harry Richmond." The latter story might seem a second study on the same theme. And yet the circumstances and characters are so very different, the imaginative conception so new and original, that we have no sense of sameness; and in fact, the second study does carry the idea much farther, does enlarge and illuminate the category of snobs.

Harry Richmond's father is the character that corresponds to the Countess de Saldar. Richmond Roy, as he daringly calls himself, is here the general directing a campaign for the social advancement of the hero. Richmond Roy is a far more attractive personality than Louisa Harrington. But he is none the less an impostor, a charlatan, deceiving and self-deceived,—a man thoroughly abandoned to false views of life. He believes himself to be of royal birth. The regular remittances that come to him through his lawyers he regards as hush money from the government. He is oblivious of the ignominy of his illegitimate birth, and his actress-mother is glorified, not degraded, by the idea of her royal connection.

Richmond Roy is not the first man to boast of descent by the left side. We know what Citizen Meredith thinks of aristocratic titles; and we might fancy in the person of Richmond Roy a sly travesty of the whole system. This romance is not conceived in the vein of "Graustark."

Richmond Roy has for his grand aim the recognition of his royal birth, and the social vindication of his son. Any courtly art is not too low for him to practise in the accomplishment of these worthy objects. His son first discovers him after the interval of separation in boyhood, on a picturesque eminence in High Germany, cased in bronze varnish, posing as an equestrian statue of a German prince. This feat was but one of many activities of Harry's father in his rôle of professional entertainer, or court buffoon. In the pursuit of a princess for his son, Richmond Roy stoops to means not consistent with the honor of a true gentleman. He practically traps his princess; lures her to England with exaggerated representation of Richie's illness, compromises her in the newspapers, and tries to force her family into consent to the marriage with Richie. Comic justice is meted out to him. He over-reaches himself. The very force employed by Richie's father in his behalf leads to the be-

trothal of Ottilia to his German rival. The un-
scrupulous player is stalemated in his own game.

A terrible blow to the ambitions of Richmond
Roy; but a more terrible one has been delivered
just before. His whole card-castle is shaken
down by the discovery of the mysterious source
of his income. It is not at all a conscious government tacitly acknowledging his claims, but an
infatuated lady, his wife's sister, poor Dorothy
Beltham, devoting her income to the sustainment
of his dreams. He is doubly shamed, at discover-
ing the weak foundations of his royal hope, and
at owing to a woman he has wronged the fuel
for his meteoric career.

Harry Richmond had to struggle all along
against the unwholesome influence of his father.
In money matters he tried to bring him to honest
sobriety. But Richmond Roy was incapable of
looking upon the truth, of seeing things uncolored
by the rosy medium of his imagination. When
Richie told his father of Squire Beltham's ulti-
matum as to his debts, and insisted on their
facing the facts, his father recommended wine to
his overwrought son. For a long while he ex-
patiated on the cordial values of wine, trying to
force some upon Richie. When his son refused
to drink, he was called unfilial, unjust. "He

sent his man Tollingby for the oldest wine in his cellar: a wine by no possibility paid for, I reflected in the midst of his praises of the wine. This buying and husbanding of choice wine upon a fictitious credit struck me as a key to his whole career." [1]

Richmond Roy was doubly deceived: he was deceived as to actual fact, and he was deceived as to the true values in life. The latter is the more radical error, and the source of all that is significant in the comedy. He spent his life, and wasted his character, in the pursuit of things of no worth. The dyer's hand was subdued to what it worked in. This case was different from that of the Harringtons. The Richmonds were not seeking an entrance into good society. They already commanded the resources of wealth, and might enjoy all the amenities of refinement and breeding. It was a dignity without meaning they sought; the satisfaction of no human appetite but unwholesome vanity. The ambition of Richmond Roy was of the pure essence of snobbery: snobbery not in its more gross and adulterated forms, but distilled, sublimated.

---

[1] Quoted from the original form of the story in the "Cornhill Magazine" (vol. XXIV), from chap. XLIV, "A first struggle with my father," which follows XLIII, "I become one of the chosen of the nation."

And it was a distilled and sublimated snobbery
that endangered the rôle of hero in the case of
Harry Richmond himself. In his case, it was
not the breath of his being. He caught the disease by contagion from his father. It did not
rage in him too furiously, and he was completely
cured in the end. But he was an imaginative
youth, his father's son. When, therefore, he had
the poetic vision of the Princess Ottilia, it was
not difficult for his father to sow in him the seed
of romantic aspiration. He was rendered proof
against the more homely charms of Janet. Perhaps it may not be necessary to attribute this to
the effect of the German experience. Janet was
the friend of his boyhood, and she was the embodiment of plain health and downright simplicity. The heart of youth craves mystery. It
is no disparagement of Ottilia's charm to say that
her rank and strangeness shed upon her the
glamor indispensable to the young man's heart.
And he could not himself deny, while yet he
aimed at the Princess, that he "had partly, in-
sensibly clung to the vain glitter of hereditary
distinction, his father's pitfall; taking it for a
substantial foothold." Richie would no doubt
have seen more clearly himself had not his father
fostered in him the false tendency. "Had not

my father succeeded in inspiring the idea that I
was something more than something?   The tendency of young men is to conceive it for themselves without assistance; a prolonged puff from
the breath of another is nearly sure to make them
mad as kings."

The Princess once removed from view, Richie
could appreciate the charm of Janet.   His vision
was restored to normality.[1]

In Harry Richmond, the snobbish instinct was
complicated by youthful sentimentalism.   A still
larger part is played by sentiment in the snobbery
of the Pole ladies in "Sandra Belloni."   They
fall more properly in the next chapter, and will
there receive more extended consideration.   We
have here to comment upon their social aspirations.   Clyde   Fitch   would   call   these   ladies
"climbers."   "Mounting"   was   the   designation

---

[1] In the original form of the story, Richie is made to appear in a somewhat ridiculous light in relation to Janet, on
his return from the Orient to find her engaged to Edbury.
He now assumes that Janet is bound to him, and accuses her
of infidelity.   Two chapters not retained are devoted to
the "raving sophistries" and "bounding paradoxes" by
which he persuades even Janet that she "may be a little
guilty"; and one chapter to his subjugation by her nobility.   These chapters are interesting as exemplification of
Meredith's comic method in the analysis of self-deception
in even his favorite characters, in the reflection of mocking
light upon them from their own acts.   But they are left
out, presumably, as not in keeping with the character of
Richie and as a confusion of the main issue.

given by the Poles themselves to their activities.
These ladies were altogether conscious of their
native tendency to mount; they were like the
element of fire banished to the depths, that seeks
its home in the empyrean. Hence the frigid
society manner on which they prided themselves.
"The ladies of Brookfield had let it be known
that, in their privacy together, they were Pole,
Polar and North Pole. Pole, Polar and North
Pole were designations of the three shades of
distance which they could convey in a bow: a
form of salute they cherished as peculiarly their
own; being a method they had invented to
rebuke the intrusiveness of the outer world, and
hold away all strangers until approved worthy."
Hence the importance they attributed to the fact
that, at his first appearance at their dinner-
table, the indigent organist exhibited perfect
evening uniform. Lady Gosstre was the social
model of the Poles. In view of the freedom from
material considerations on which they plumed
themselves, one is a little surprised at the physical
detail marked by them among other points as
making the distinction of that lady. Lady
Gosstre's carriage of her shoulders was admitted
to be worthy of study. In this, we are reminded
of the instructions given by Richmond Roy and

the Countess de Saldar to their pupils. "The main things," according to one general, "are to be able to stand well, walk well, and look with an eye at home in its socket." Evan's task, the Harrington sisters agreed, was "to learn the management of his mouth, how to dress his shoulders, and to direct his eyes."

It is points like these that emphasize the comic character of the snob. The desire for wealth is natural enough, and can be made comic only when, as in the "Miser," the uses of wealth are forgotten in an exclusive passion for the gold itself. The desire to move among persons of refinement and to be free from the intrusions of vulgarity has in it nothing reprehensible or ridiculous. What characterizes the snob is his false estimate of social values. He takes the husk for the kernel. He supposes gentility to consist in posture, gait, the manipulation of the monocle. As for the Pole ladies, they did not even have a well-defined notion of the advantages for which they slaved. They showed too much heat. They did protest too much. They were incapable of recognizing true natural breeding when they saw it. Emilia they adopted because her voice made her a lion. It was in spite of her admirable simplicity they took her, and

with much trepidation. They did not realize
that education and refinement are their own pass-
ports. This is the radical error of the snob,
whether in high life or low life.

The true doctrine that arises from the whole
of the Book of Snobs finds statement in "Evan
Harrington." Evan maintained his place among
gentlefolk even after the full discovery of his
birth and occupation, as his father had done
before him. "In this struggle with society,"
says the author, with only a shade of irony, and
that not for Evan, "I see one of the instances
where success is entirely to be honored and remains a proof of merit. For however boldly
antagonism may storm the ranks of society, it
will certainly be repelled, whereas affinity cannot
be resisted; and they who, against obstacles of
birth, claim and keep their position among the
educated and refined, have that affinity."

CHAPTER V

WE now part company with Dickens and Thackeray, and enter the peculiar realm of Meredith. From this point on, we consider comic studies more subtle and searching than are required by the superficial vice of snobbery. The whole conception of the sentimentalist as an object of comic treatment is one of the most original of Meredith's contributions to the English novel. Here we come to the heart of his comic method. Nowhere does he apply more penetrating criticism to what we think most valid and substantial in our own civilized nature.

In our progress from brutal to spiritual beings, the push forward, the lift upward, is given us by our ideals. We are guided not wholly now by animal instinct, but by certain general conceptions of beauty, fitness, social expediency. Thence come law, morality, the principles of beauty, the dignity of character. We pride ourselves on our emancipation from material fact.

86

Meredith is the last person to disparage the civilizing process. He takes it for granted, as the one thing worth while, the meaning and purpose of life. But he makes it his business to point out certain maladies incident to the state of half-civilization, maladies resulting in fact from an abuse of the very ideals by which civilization is made possible. The sentimentalist, in Meredith's usage, is one whose ideals are his undoing, because they are not related to fact. He puts on the wings of Icarus, and leaves the solid earth only to be dropped again wingless into the abyss. True feeling is the most precious thing in life; but a false sentiment, put on for ornament, or taken up for plaything, is perilous and an object of laughter.

Sentimentality is a finer form of snobbery. One variety of snob consists of those who suppose themselves, or affect, to be of greater social importance than they are. It is an affair of wealth and family, of circumstances external to the man. The sentimentalist is a spiritual snob. He supposes himself to be possessed of insights and emotions more rare than the ordinary. He puts on a pharisaic robe of sentiment, makes broad his phylacteries, and thanks God he is not as other men are. There was a touch of the senti-

mentalist in Harry Richmond, a fair representative of imaginative youth. This and snobbery
combined with mere love of strangeness to bind
him to his father's scheme of marrying a princess.
Sentiment underlay the snobbery of General
Ople. The snobbery of the Pole ladies was a
variety of sentimentalism. In all these cases,
the sentimentalist, conscious of a spiritual superiority, wished to put upon it the seal of social
ascendancy. Snobbery was here the outward
manifestation of a more radical self-deception
within the private court. The snob is concerned
about his valuation in the social world, the
sentimentalist about his valuation in the world
of feeling.

The sentimentalist makes his appearance rather
often in the pages of Meredith.[1] Sir Austin was

[1] The lover of comedy can never forgive Meredith for
leaving unfinished ;that delicious tantalizing fragment of
comic play, the "Sentimentalists." Professor Spiral's admirers belong, like the Pole sisters, to those who cultivate
the nice feelings and the fine shades. And their superior
and leader, the "dedicated widow," was destined to be one
of the most refined and delectable of all sentimentalists.
Already, in her relations to Arden, in the first act, one is
aware of an ironic contrast of character suggestive of that
in the "Misanthrope."

Perhaps Captain Con of "Celt and Saxon" is meant for
one variety of sentimentalist. The reader will be able to
mention various sentimentalists whom I do not consider
individually, such as the Duvidney ladies in "One of Our
Conquerors." "Vittoria," though it continues the story
of Wilfrid Pole and Emilia, does not add anything appre-
ciable to the picture of the sentimentalist.

something of a sentimentalist. We shall find elements of the vice in Victor Radnor and Fleetwood. But our present concern is with a book devoted almost wholly to sentimental types, Meredith's third novel, "Sandra Belloni."

Under the chapter-head "The Tragedy of Sentiment," and in the person of Sir Purcell Barrett, Meredith here gives us sentimentalism in a nutshell. This gentleman, doomed to poverty by the arbitrary whim of his father, is a victim of hard luck—or what he likes to consider such. From his earliest years, a personal pride has made him turn his back resolutely on fact, and has prevented him from the expression of complaint against injustice. He is too delicate to complain of his own father, and too proud to admit insanity in his own family. He prefers to attribute his father's madness to the fates themselves. He is conscious of his own merits, his own fineness of feeling, and exaltation of ideals; and on the other hand, of the misfortune heaped upon him—he must believe—by Fate or Providence. It is like the Ordeal of the Feverels. The world itself is out of joint: it does not measure up to his standard of justice and nobility. When he encounters Cornelia Pole, he has a revival of hope. Her he clothes with his ideal, and determines to make trial in her person of this order of things. If she proves worthy, his faith may lean on her for support; if not, he must yield to despair. Unfortunately he is not strong in faith; and he is obliged, in order to give himself confidence, to endow the lady of the test with "unexampled virtues." Having done so, he is incapable of making any compromise with actuality. When the lady proves human, subject to the stresses and strains of complex social life, he can make no effort to understand or excuse her shortcomings. He will not even put them into words, so that they may be discussed. Cornelia Pole is likewise a sentimentalist, and equally averse to an honest discussion of their relations. She means in the end to satisfy her ideal and the man she loves; but in the meantime, serving the world for her father's sake, she expects her lover to "understand." His failure to do so—his wilful blindness, we might call it—leads to his despair, and to suicide. This is the final luxury of sentiment.

The sentimentalist is not much alive at the heart. The weakness of that organ is made up for by the strong activity of the fancy. Love and fancy were synonyms in the playful language of Elizabethan amorous poets. And they recog-

nized how little share the heart has in the breeding of fanciful love.

> "Tell me where is fancy bred,
> Or in the heart, or in the head?"

Fancy, wherever engendered, is with the true
sentimentalist a tyrant. He believes in the
divine right of this king, and on regicide he looks
with horror. Rather than compromise an ideal,
he will turn his face away from life. Which
means that he is degenerate, not much alive. It
is not this kind of men that forward the movement of our race. Ideals are for them the chariot
of the sun, and they mad Phaëton. And yet
they are a product of the civilizing process; they
are in fact in the vanguard of the movement.
For they are idealists, though misguided.

Purcell Barrett is but an incidental and subordinate study in the sentimentalism represented
more extensively by the Pole family. Both the
sisters and Wilfrid Pole belong to this category;
but it is convenient to consider them separately,
as the difference of sex and circumstance involves
a considerable difference in the manifestation of
the vice.

The aspiration of the Pole ladies was not merely
for social prestige. That was an incident and an

outward seal to the less easily definable superiority they cultivated.   They were "aiming at they knew not exactly what, save that it was something so wide that it had not a name, and so high in the air that no one could see it."   This was what troubled the Tinleys, equally bent on social advancement.   The Pole ladies were unintelligible to them.   "To dress well, to be refined, to marry well—I understand all that perfectly; but who *could* understand *them?* Not they themselves, I am certain."   It was this unintelligible quality, this vague superiority of theirs, that made them feel unembarrassed in the contemplation of aristocrats.   They were not afraid of Lady Gosstre.   They "allowed themselves to bow to her with the greater humility, owing to the secret sense they nursed of overtopping her still in that ineffable Something which they alone possessed: a casket little people will be wise in not hurrying our Father Time to open for them, if they would continue to enjoy the jewel they suppose it to contain."

This ineffable Something consisted in a special niceness of feeling, a special fineness of perception and expression, pursued by these ladies.   They were seeking to scale society by patronizing the fine arts.   The Misses Pole are the kind of ladies

who form circles for the study of Browning, and
of Meredith himself, in order, like the Pharisee,
to signalize their separateness.   The word *culture*
is not mentioned, so far as I can remember; but
that word, pronounced Bostonese with an *h* for
an *r*, will convey to the American reader a sense
of what they meant.   The gradual and incom-
plete mastery of the word "eclectic" by Adela
Pole, with her allusion to "æsthetic" as a word
already current among the sisters, suggests the
element of the precious in their ideals of speech
and taste.   Arabella's unsuccessful attempt to
give Mr. Pericles a notion of "soul" in the moon
indicates the poetic superiority that went along
with the linguistic.   But the sisters were most
remarkable for the delicacy of their sentiment in
relation to one another, the care with which any
vulgar or mercenary motive was excluded from
their minds, and the ingenuity with which even
the plainest matter of fact was conveyed in elegant periphrasis, by implication or adumbration.
They played with each other, and so far as possible with all the world, the self-flattering game of
Nice Feelings and Fine Shades.

They tried to impose their dream upon the
actual world.   They would not use their eyes for
the perception of anything unpleasant.   Ugly

facts they kept out of their contemplation by not framing them in speech. They preferred to spare themselves pain. "They paved the future with gold, and, if I may use so bold a figure, lifted parasols against the great sun that was to shine upon them." The comedy lies in the removal of the parasol.

In their dislike for vulgar fact, they naturally included that most central of all vulgarities, the question of supplies. The consideration of money they regarded as beneath the dignity of beings devoted to the cultivation of the Nice Feelings. They were under the impression that their father was rich; but this fact they did not count in estimating their own importance. They did indeed congratulate themselves on their country home of Brookfield, and they were exerting themselves to persuade their father to purchase the more imposing place of Besworth. But they were resolutely set against translating these social advantages into terms of lucre. When their father stipulated on their receiving the unutterable Mrs. Chump as a condition of his securing Besworth, and when their brother Wilfrid went over to the Philistines, the sisters were brought with the utmost difficulty to perceive that money was at the bottom of all this. When

one of them came at last to a tentative acknowledg-
ment of this fact, the awful word was uttered
under a mask shamefacedly. "A voice said,
'Money!' Which of the sisters had spoken Adela
did not know. It was bitter enough that one
could be brought to utter the thing, even if her
ideas were so base as to suspect it."

These ladies did not realize how essential money
is to the cultivation of the Nice Feelings and the
Fine Shades. The sentimentalist "should reflect,
but does not, that the fine feelers by which the
iniquities of gold are so keenly discerned, are a
growth due to it, nevertheless. Those 'fine
feelers,' or antennæ of the senses, come of sweet
ease; that is synonymous with gold in our island-
latitude." Not only are the Fine Shades impossible save on a golden background; they become
ridiculous without it. As Wilfrid Pole rather
brutally put it to his sisters, "If you posture, and
are poor, you provoke ridicule."

This fact they come to realize during the year
in which their comedy is enacting. Gradually
there grows in the depths of their consciousness
the ill-defined dread sense of this vulgar monster
threatening. Martha Chump is a sort of physical
embodiment of the mysterious fact; and there is
a bitter irony in the circumstance that this

woman, whom they so abhor and finally drive
from the house, is the source of that very security
in which the Nice Feelings grow. The mere contact of such a woman was bad enough. The
Fine Shades languished in the presence of one so
plain-spoken, so wanting in all delicacy of breeding. It was fatal to the Nice Feelings to witness
the vulgar and open wooing of their father by the
relict of Alderman Chump, and her consumption
of wine in his company after dinner. It was
excruciating to refined ears to listen to her brogue
and her anecdotes. After her banishment the
sisters were condemned to the invention of lies
in order to save their father. The invention of
lies is the natural business of the sentimentalist;
but not of lies recognized as such, misrepresenta-
tion of plain matters of fact. Matters of fact
are too vulgar a material upon which to exercise
the idealizing faculty. It is plain that, in this
occupation, the ladies of Brookfield had left far
behind the realm of the Fine Shades and the Nice
Feelings.

But while they were inventing lies for their
father, they were acting lies to one another, and to
their several lovers. Cornelia, while she really
loved one man, and was determined in her heart
to give herself to him at last, felt obliged, on her

father's account, to keep on the string another more promising suitor. She did not know that the more promising suitor had discovered her preference, and had transferred his interest to her sister Adela. Arabella continued to play off her two lovers against one another, unwilling to relinquish either, and in danger—as it seemed to Adela—of losing both. Adela, while now supposed to be engaged to her own Captain, had not long since made love to one of Arabella's lovers, and was at present making love to one of Cornelia's. The only one of the three that had a real affection was Cornelia, and that was not strong enough to make itself a material fact. Arabella and Adela are rather pale characters; but if they are to be distinguished, Arabella seemed to flirt for the fun of flirting, while Adela appears to have had a more business-like eye for social advantages connected with a husband. Adela is the only one that in the sequel, "Vittoria," turns up married. But in the present story she was doomed to disappointment through the meanness of her sister Cornelia. After the suicide of Purcell Barrett, Adela showed her genius for strategy in desiring Cornelia not to wear mourning. There was yet a good chance that Sir Twickenham would take Adela; unless

indeed Cornelia should persist in displaying the
garb of sorrow, and so frightening away a man
sensitive to ridicule and vulgar tattle. But
Cornelia does persist; and Adela is shown us in
the end with soured visage, waiting, listening in
vain for the footsteps of the man.

All this, understand, is "translated out of the
Fine Shades." None of the ladies would have
phrased the facts quite in this naked, vulgar
fashion. None of them would have allowed in
her most inner consciousness so low interpretation of her acts. But the stress of a vulgar
world was leading them to admissions of fact
quite contrary to their sentimental assumptions;
and they were all acting in ways plainly dishonest, and in palpable opposition to their expressed ideals. Tested by the outward and the
inner fact, their sentiments were false or worthless.

In this comedy of the sisters Pole, the author
at times permits the clown to show his silly face.
He was aware of danger from that insuppressible
farceur, as he reminds us at the beginning.
"After thus stating to you the vast pretensions
of the ladies of Brookfield, it would be unfair to
sketch their portraits. Nothing but comedy
bordering on burlesque could issue from the contrast, though they graced a drawing-room, or a

pew, and had properly elegant habits and taste
in dress, and were all fair to the sight." But the
ladies were allowed themselves to draw the
ludicrous contrast by their speech and acts. It
may be the author was too anxious at times lest
the reader should put faith in the pretensions of
the sentimentalist. The result is a want of the
fineness that marks the comedy of his later
books. In the third novel of Meredith we can
still discern the influence of "Joseph Andrews"
or "Pickwick Papers." But here we should note
a distinction. There is a graded scale of the
ludicrous in Meredith's representation of sentimentalism as well as in that of snobbery. Cornelia is intended, I think, to be somewhat separate
from the ridicule that falls upon her cruder sisters.
In her the reader can take a certain sympathetic
interest. And yet it was her practice of the common art that did most harm. No vice becomes
less vicious for being more refined.

And now for their brother. A less broadly
comic figure than his sisters is Wilfrid Pole, for
he does not in large degree share their euphuism;
and, besides, we have represented in him sentiment in process of development into true passion.
But the uncertainty of feeling is more ridiculous
in the active, initiatory male. And it is long

before we see evidences of the transformation.
Wilfrid is one of the men who like to play with
love because it illuminates them and gives them
an agreeable sense of emotion.   It makes a pleasant appeal to vanity and pride.   But this love is
not of the serious kind that goes straight to its
mark, that strives to make itself fact.   It is a ster-
ile flower, that blooms for itself and bears no fruit.

And above all, it is not a robust feeling; but
keenly sensitive to any breath of ridicule, any
suggestion of the commonplace.   The sentimentalist is most fastidious, most critical of the object
of his love, lest his ideal be sullied in her.   His
senses are super-refined, incapable of supporting
the impact of harsh reality.   Wilfrid's ideal for a
woman was "extreme refinement . . . even up
to the thin edge of inanity."   And it was his fate
to feel the attraction of extreme simplicity in the
person of Emilia.   Never so addicted to the Fine
Shades as his sisters, and being of the opposite
sex, he could feel more than they the charm of
this uncultivated and unconventional creature.
But he was destined to many a struggle with his
fastidious senses before he could yield his heart
to one so wanting in artificial refinements.
Emilia's naïve recital of her history was a series
of shocks to his sensibilities.   The bohemian life

with her father in London, the poverty and po-
tatoes, the meeting with the strange man in the
park, the "Jew gentleman"—these were blows
fatal to the dainty thing his feeling was. On a
later occasion, when Emilia sang for the country
fellows, and had to be rescued from the fight that
ensued between the rival clubs, Wilfrid's sentiment was frightened away by the ridiculous
affair, and it required moonlight and nightingales
to lure it back again.

In the scene that followed, the sentimentalist
was a little frightened by the actuality of love
displayed by the lady. The dilettantism of his
feeling is contrasted with the intense seriousness
of hers,—which flattered him and worried him
at once. Fortunately, on the next morning, he
was saved by a displeasing memory. He recalled
that, after the scene in the smoking-booth,
Emilia's hair was redolent of pipe-smoke. His
love was not equal to such a test, and "much
gold leaf," we are told, "peeled away from her
image in his heart."

But the sentimentalist cannot escape the passion he has inspired in the natural woman. It is
Emilia that seeks out her lover at Lady Charlotte's and summons him home. It is she that
proposes the earnest question of marriage. That

was not the goal of the sentimentalist. He cannot afford to turn his sentiment into that sort of fact. Social considerations are against it in this case. His father requires that he support the tottering prestige of the family by marrying Lady Charlotte, to whom he is practically engaged. Wilfrid "diplomatizes" with most comic indecision, laying the blame for his backwardness on his father. He comes later to realize that Emilia is in need of protection; and now he has begun actually to *love* that winning creature. He is now not merely embarrassed: he is in danger. He strives to root out a passion so opposed to his interests. The next moment he has yielded, and we find him making a ludicrous vain effort to get released from Lady Charlotte by confession of his indigence. His indecision continues. The two women, unashamed of their love, struggle for the mastery. There comes the scene in which he is led to declare his love for Lady Charlotte and repudiate Emilia. Lady Charlotte, too, has charms. The philanderer grows hungry. It requires protestations to pierce the lady's armor of chaste reserve. Wilfrid protests that he loves only Lady Charlotte; that he does not love Emilia, and has never loved her. The protestations are overheard by Emilia.

The last act of this comedy shows the feelings of Wilfrid and Emilia reversed. Her love for him is destroyed by his determination to fight her fatherland, against the cause of liberty. It is he now that begins to feel actual passion while she nurses mere sentiment. The last scene of his comic acting is when Emilia delivers a stroke of practical repartee at Lady Charlotte. Emilia leads Wilfrid to declare his love for herself, and his want of love for Lady Charlotte, with the same emphasis with which he had formerly made the exactly converse declaration. And Lady Charlotte is by to hear. Lady Charlotte gives up her claim on him; Emilia is off for Italy. Both ladies give him up. It is comic justice.

Meantime we have had an exhibition of senti- mental heroics. During Emilia's sojourn in Wales, the sentiment of Wilfrid has become rampant, uncontrollable. It has taken on the semblance of real passion, and might have been mistaken for that were it not for the author's warnings.[1] The sentimentalist, he tells us, is capable of creating for himself, out of his cher- ished images and sensations, a sort of monster that lifts him up and hurries him off on mad career through the sky. Hippogriff he calls this

[1] In chapters XLIV, XLV and LI.

pseudo-passion or sur-excited Sentiment.   It is
still that fanciful creature seeking the gratification of its artificially developed tastes, not the
natural instinct seeking its natural satisfaction.
It alternately raises him to giddy heights and
dashes him down to the pit, as he gains or loses
faith in his own feeling.   It is, moreover, at
variance with common sense, will take cogni-
zance of no barriers in the way of desire, will not
even consider where it is going: whereas true
passion has ever a goal which it seeks with the
guidance of good sense.   When Wilfrid started
for Wales in pursuit of his Emilia, he would not
consider what were the practical consequences he
had in view.   "What then did this pursuit of
Emilia mean?   To blink this question, he had to
give the spur to Hippogriff.   It meant (upon
Hippogriff at a brisk gallop), that he intended to
live for her, die for her, if need be, and carve
out of the world all that she would require."
But he would not take the trouble to consider
whether it meant marriage.

Matter of fact continues to be the one thing
avoided by the idle sentimentalist.   It is this
that constitutes the family likeness of Wilfrid,
his sisters and Cornelia's lover.   Purcell Barrett
would rather die in his delicacy than make com-

promise with human fact in his beloved. The
Pole sisters ignored as long as it was possible the
vulgar circumstances in which they found themselves involved; and while they could act from
motives selfish and mean, they could not bring
themselves to frame in words, or even to con-
template, the truth of these acts and motives.
Both they and Wilfrid trifled with love, not
wishing to understand its practical implications.
Wilfrid, through most of his career, could appreciate Emilia only when he had divested her of
the natural, and had dressed her out in his own
sentimental ideal.

Emilia is the heroine of this story. In the
comedy she serves as a foil for the unnatural
Poles, brother and sisters. Another foil is Mrs.
Chump, ridiculous enough on the surface, but
chiefly on the surface. Ignorance and vulgarity
are ridiculous not in themselves but in their setting. We find them funny in people of means
moving in refined society, irrepressible and unconscious of disqualifications. Mrs. Chump is at
least perfectly natural: there is no affectation,
snobbish or sentimental, to invite the malice of
the comic imps. The ridiculousness of the Poles
strikes deeper; its root is an absurdity in character. Another set of persons would seem to

have been introduced mainly as another foil to
them. Merthyr and Georgiana are devoted to
the cause of Italian independence, ready to make
every sacrifice for what they have at heart.
Quixotic their countrymen would call these
altruists. Practical idealists they are. Meredith
wishes it clear that he is not making fun of ideals,
of noble practical sentiment. At the end of a
very affecting dialogue between these enthusi-
asts, the author remarks: "A sentimental pair
likewise, if you please; but these were sentimentalists who served an active deity, and not
that arbitrary projection of a subtle selfishness
which rules the fairer portion of our fat England."

One chapter offers us a fantastic Rabelaisian
symbol of sentimentalism. The hero is presented
running madly down a London street, in pursuit
of the heroine in a carriage. Colliding with a
pot-boy, he is drenched with beer from throat
to knee. When he overtakes the lady, he realizes
that the smell of bad beer is not fit for the nose
of a heroine. Providence appears with a bottle
of Alderman's Bouquet, Mrs. Chump's perfume;
and one smell is set to expel the other. Alderman's Bouquet does not suggest the rarest of
odors; and we have, in any case, two fragrances

for one. The hero does not attempt to interview
the heroine. "The Philosopher, up to this point
rigidly excluded, rushes forward to the footlights
to explain in a note, that Wilfrid, thus setting a
perfume to contend with a stench, instead of
waiting for time, change of raiment, and the
broad lusty airs of heaven to blow him fresh
again, symbolizes the vice of Sentimentalism, and
what it is always doing. Enough!" [1]

[1] This symbol of sentimentalism is a favorite of Meredith's. It recurs in the chapter about the lapdog Tasso in
"One of Our Conquerors," and in "Celt and Saxon" in relation to Mrs. Captain Con, who stands, it would seem, for
the downright honesty of the Saxon as opposed to the
musky sentiment of the Celt. "I must hurry and wash my
hair," says Capt. Con, going to the embrace of his lady
from indulgence in nicotine; "She can't bear a perfume to
kill a stink; she carries her charitable heart that far."
There is apparently some similar intention in the concluding *jeu d'esprit* of "Farina." But humorous symbolism
in Meredith should have a chapter to itself.

CHAPTER VI

THE OPTIMIST

CLOSE of kin to the sentimentalist is the optimist by virtue of his fondness for pleasant illusions, his disinclination to criticism. I have not in mind a theoretical optimism like that of the "Essay on Man," consistent with the most vicious application of the critical spirit to human nature. The optimist here considered is the optimist by temperament. Being inclined to a rosy view of things by a happy disposition, his heart is pledged to a faith in his world as the best possible of all worlds. His mind is called into requisition only for supporting argument, and is promptly snubbed on the betrayal of any critical tendency. He will not harbor disquieting intrusive suggestions; and will sometimes walk straight into a storm-cloud rather than acknowledge the presence of danger. Upon his own character he turns the same flattering light; and hence proves capable of acts hardly justifiable in the best possible of worlds.

Such an optimist is Victor Radnor, central figure of "One of Our Conquerors." Being naturally formed for happiness, he does not wish to learn of anything likely to obscure a cheerful view of himself or the cosmos. He hates satire by natural instinct. His faculty is for the rosy rhetorical. He is capable of dispersing trouble with a song. In letters and music, his taste is for the unreflective, the stirring, the melodious and declamatory. He is given to stimulants, physical and intellectual. Simple activity is the chief of these; but wine is thrown in to suggest the true character of the activity. The Old Veuve that occupies the third and fourth chapters of the story serves to symbolize, like the wine in "Harry Richmond," the refracting and colored medium through which the self-deceiver views his world. Victor Radnor has much of the childlike charm of Richmond Roy. He was loved by those who read his character; and we delight in his flowering, benevolent nature while we learn the comic lessons of his career.

But he is obliged to be an actor, an "histrionic self-deceiver." He has to deceive others and himself as to his own motives and the actual status of his affairs. For he must at all times affirm that all is right with him. And he has to strangle

every suggestion to the contrary. Thus he interprets his motives for marrying Mrs. Burman.

"Colney Durance accused him of entering into
bonds with somebody's grandmother for the
simple sake of browsing on her thousands: a
picture of himself too abhorrent to Victor to
permit of any sort of acceptance. Consequently
he struck away to the other extreme of those who
have a choice in mixed motives: he protested
that compassion had been the cause of it. Looking at the circumstance now, he could see, allowing for human frailty—perhaps a wish to join
the ranks of the wealthy—compassion for the
woman for the principal motive. How often
had she not in those old days praised his generosity for allying his golden youth to her withered
age—Mrs. Burman's very words."

Thus refined nature tempers for the sentimentalist the keen wind of truth. Again the mental
processes of the optimist are anatomized in the
following reflections of Victor on the same topic.

"Naturally he was among the happiest of
human creatures; he willed it so, with consent
of circumstances; a boisterous consent, as when
votes are reckoned for a favourite candidate:
excepting on the part of a small band of black
dissentients in a corner, a minute opaque body,
devilish in their irreconcilability, who maintain
their struggle to provoke discord, with a cry
disclosing the one error of his youth, the sole
bad step chargeable upon his antecedents. But
do we listen to them? Shall we not have them
turned out? He gives the sign for it; and he

leaves his buoying constituents to outroar them;
and he tells a friend that it was not, as one may
say, an error, although an erratic step: but let
us explain to our bosom friend; it was a step
quite unregretted, gloried in"; etc.

Victor Radnor is set up for a type of the
sentimental optimist. And he is assigned a
critic and opponent who stands for the pessimist.[1] Throughout their careers, Victor Radnor,
man of affairs, and Colney Durance, man of
letters, were engaged in a sort of shadowy debate, in which they continued to maintain "those
gosling affirmatives and negatives," as Meredith
calls the two extreme views of life prevailing in
the nineteenth century. And Colney Durance
was able, in the end, to say "I told you so" to
the tragic refutation of Victor's shallow theory.
Victor was an optimist in regard to public affairs
as well as private. London raised him to exulta-
tion with its splendid confusion of trade, the
sense of movement and power, the magnificent
turbulent scenery of street and river. He took
no stock in Colney's criticisms of the English
nation. If she had not the brains and method
of Germany, she had strength and earnestness

[1] For the references to optimism and pessimism, see especially chapters XIX, XX, XLII. Observe also what
Meredith says of optimism and pessimism as a subject of
comedy in the "Essay on Comedy."

bound to prevail. If Colney prophesied the subjugation of the slothful, luxurious Saxon by the
energetic Jew, Victor had an Idea for the social
rehabilitation of the Saxon.

It was a vague idea that eluded definition.
Victor found and lost it one day while crossing
London bridge; and it took him a whole year,
searching in the corners of his brain, to recover
it. On the day of his great undelivered speech,
it was perfectly clear to him. It is not quite so
clear to us from the rapid sketch with which he
favored his friend while on the way to the lec-
ture-hall. And Mr. Radnor's own practice seems
strangely at variance with his theory. In his
remarks to Fenellan there appears more than a
touch of inconsequence. "Great fortunes now,"
says the very wealthy man, "are becoming the
giants of old to stalk the land; or the mediæval
Barons. Dispersion of wealth is the secret.
Nataly's of that mind with me. A decent poverty! She's rather wearying, wants a change.
I've a steam-yacht in my eye, for next month on
the Mediterranean. All our set. She likes quiet.
I believe in my political recipe for it." There
seems to be no question in his mind about
the consistency of steam-yachts with a decent
poverty.

The relation of Victor's Idea to his optimism may not be immediately apparent. He who is sufficiently aware of sickness to propose a remedy does not well answer to the definition of optimist. But Victor would never have been brought to admit a malady save by the insistence of his satirical friend; and the optimistic temperament is displayed in his manner of disposing of an unpleasant suggestion. He blinds and flatters himself with the pretence that he has an Idea, a sovereign remedy for all the ills of his own and the public life. The Idea is too vague for intelligible statement; and so far as it does make itself understood, it is seen to be at variance with his own practice. Just as Sir Austin's want of science is the more striking in view of his scientific pretensions, so Victor's poverty of thought is set off more pointedly by the fuss he makes over this Idea. "Definition," says the author, dryly, "seemed to be an extirpating enemy to this idea." The author suggests that Mr. Radnor lacked reasoning powers, or that they were submerged by his feelings. This predominance of feelings over the critical faculties marks the sentimental optimist.

Victor's lieutenant Skepsey seems intended to throw light upon him somewhat as Jack Raikes

threw light upon Evan Harrington. Skepsey
was as ardent a patriot as his chief, as optimistic
with regard to the future of England. And he
looked for Saxon success in a direction similar
to that contemplated by Mr. Radnor. Radnor
trusted in England's native energy and strength.
Skepsey, more specific, looked upon the manly
art of boxing and its military counterpart as the
guarantee of English supremacy. The waggish
author even killed off the little man's wife on
purpose to give him a more appropriate mate in
a member of the Salvation Army,—a militant
lady opposed on religious principle to war and
fisticuffs. Neither Skepsey nor Mr. Radnor included brains in his prescription for England's
sickness. *Physical* training is all that Skepsey
had in mind. His appeal to the boxing glove
would seem to be a humorous counterpart of
something in his master's optimism.

According to Victor, the optimist is naturally
given to action. "The Optimist, impelled by his
exuberant anticipatory trustfulness, is an author,
and does things; whereas the Pessimist is your
chaired critic, with the delivery of a censor, generally an undoer of things." Accordingly Victor
Radnor was a man of affairs. He was a practical
optimist, a conqueror. The word conqueror

recurs rather frequently in Meredith for the
semi-satirical designation of a certain type of
flourishing man.[1] In the "Egoist," in the "Tale
of Chloe," in the "Tragic Comedians," it is used
of the men vulgarly known as lady-killers, or in
Meredith's description, "the race of amorous
heroes who glory in pursuing, overtaking, sub-
duing." Lady Camper says of General Ople that
he "nursed the absurd idea of being one of our
conquerors." This phrase Meredith uses now as
the title of a novel. But while Victor Radnor is
"one of our conquerors" in the limited sense
intended by Lady Camper, while he was formed
by nature for ascendancy over the gentler sex,
the term has in his case a wider embrace. It
was not merely the sex over which he made his
triumphs, but the world. He was victor in
business, in society, among the people, in poli-
tics. He was what we call a captain of industry.
He was a leader of men.

He was indeed "one of the embodied elements,
hot from Nature's workshop." He was a man
running over with energies that must be em-

[1] "Egoist," XXII, compare XXXV; "Chloe," VII;
"Tragic Comedians," V; "One of Our Conquerors," IX,
XIII. Compare chapter-head of XXXI; "conquered
world" in XXVII; "He conquered Nataly" in VI; and
the Christian name of the conqueror.

ployed. He could not be content with quiet
obscurity; but was irresistibly driven from
within to conspicuous activity. His friend Colney was irritated at his "insane itch to be the
bobbing cork on the wave of the minute." His
beloved Nataly and his daughter Nesta could
not comprehend "the necessity it was for him to
mix and be foremost with the world." On the
other hand he reproached Nataly with "the void
of plot, drama, shuffle of excitement." For himself, he was a "more than Titanically audacious
balloonist." His "course was an ascension from
heights to heights."

Meantime this balloon ascension was a dangerous business. As Victor and Nataly were not
married before the law, and Victor's legal wife
was still living and threatening, it behooved
them, in common sense, to follow a more obscure
course. But the law of Victor's being required
that he should build great houses and inhabit
them, that he should bring together society and
conquer it. For the sake of Nataly and Nesta,
to be sure, but none the less for the satisfaction of
his own appetite for action. The conqueror cannot sit forever in his tent. And so he was obliged
to persuade himself of the speedy demise of Mrs.
Burman Radnor, and to impose his belief on

Nataly. And he had to shut his eyes to the evidence of Nataly's suffering. He could not understand how distressing to the sensitive woman was the social prominence in which he delighted, how the dread of scandal was constantly a strain upon her heart. Every week he looked forward to a near day when he could make her his legal wife, and her fears might cease. Meantime he would subjugate the social world, and make parliament the seat of his beneficent activities.

In the subjugation of society, the conqueror must resort to unworthy means for an object of doubtful worth. The building of Lakelands was clearly not in harmony with his great Idea of the simple life for the wealthy. And when he undertook to entrap the heir of an earldom, he was falling below the world's standard of honesty. In spite of herself, Nataly could not help judging him, when she observed the "twists of elusiveness" with which he would forward and disguise his schemes. Again we have the comic protagonist passing beneath the searching scrutiny of the intimate woman. Still more searching is the criticism of satirical Colney. He found in his friend a type of his illogical country. He had no patience with Victor for the way he ignored the failing health of Nataly. And he saw that Victor

was the slave of his object. He would hardly
acknowledge Victor's success, and he said his
was a dirty road to success.

Victor's experience leads him to reflection himself upon this theme. "Victor had yet to learn
that a man with a material object in aim, is the
man of his object; and the nearer to his mark,
often the farther is he from a sober self; he is
more the arrow of his bow than bow to his arrow.
This we pay for scheming: and success is costly;
we find we have pledged the better half of ourselves to clutch it; not to be redeemed with the
whole handful of our prize! He was, however,
learning after his leaping fashion. Nataly's de-
fective sympathy made him look at things
through the feelings she depressed." Later on,
when he had enlisted Lady Grace as an ally for
the social campaign, he was led to still more
reflection by the kind of payment he found himself making to that lady. "It moved him to
examine the poor value of his aim, by tying him
to the contemptible means. . . . His dulled
physical system asked, as with the sensations of
a man at the start from sleep in the hurrying
grip of steam, what on earth he wanted to get,
and what was the substance of his gains." Victor
received warning from the hedonist in him that

he was not enjoying himself as much as he might anticipate.

Whenever such reflections troubled him, he would fall back on his great Idea for comfort. "Somewhere he had an idea, that would lift and cleanse all degradations." His own plan of Lakelands and Dudley Sowerby was somehow bound up in the general idea for the regeneration of the English people; and all that he did was somehow means to that large end. But alas! he could never quite recover the lost idea; and moreover, he had taken, since that day, to a "morbid indulgence in reflection." He associated this with the bump made by the fall on the back of his head. "He knew well it was a fancy. But it was a fact also, that since the day of the fall (never, save in merest glimpses, before that day) he had taken to look behind him, as though an eye had been knocked in the back of his head."

In other words, the conquering optimist, heretofore bent exclusively on his own plans of conquest in the future, is invaded by a sense of what he owes to the past. The physical fall but symbolizes a jolt from circumstance. Having invoked the goddess Nature for his justification in leaving Mrs. Burman, he was under the impression that he could go ahead just as if he had never pledged

himself to the lady. He was to learn that who-
ever contracts a debt must pay it in one way or
another: that Mrs. Burman had still a claim on
him, and he could not call himself free man till
the day of her death. Victor unfortunately
learned his lesson when it was too late. His
tragic fate was his teacher. The critic had in
him a tardy birth, and was never permitted
growth to manhood.

The critic would have opened his eyes to the
paradox there was in the case of social insurgents
wooing society.[1]

The critic would have bidden him follow
Nataly's instinct for quiet and obscurity. But
his conquering spirit drove him into the fray;
and his sanguine disposition kept leading him to
suppose the battle nearly won. And thus he prolonged the agony of his beloved till she could
bear no more. His great speech was never delivered. He was called home from the theatre
to the dead body of his beloved. Her heart was
broken. A few hours later died Mrs. Burman,
having done her worst. Insanity was the only
relief for the frantic conqueror.

Colney Durance, the pessimist, took pains to
verify to the minutes the exact interval between

[1] See the chapter on the Comic Philosophy.

Nataly's death and Mrs. Burman's, struck with
the strange irony of their succession. But the
author will not have us lay the catastrophe on
the arbitrary and whimsical fates. It was the
tragic folly of Victor Radnor that killed Nataly.
A man of great charm and amiability in private
life, a man of genius in business, admirable in
action, he yet showed a want of reflective or
critical faculties that would have given balance
to his character. He fostered the growth of flattering illusory opinions; and the sanguine optimism that made him so attractive and prevailing hurried him blindly on to the tragic end.
Victor Radnor stands for the England of his
day,[1] uncritical; craving action, sensation, heart-
throbs;[2] averse to reflection; seeing everything
through the rosy medium of the blood—driving
upon disaster. Colney Durance is the critical
spirit incarnate,—fruitless, unproductive. There
must be a wedding of heart and head.

[1] See especially IX and XXI. "But these good friends
about him stood for the country, an illogical country; and
as he could not well attack his host, Victor Radnor, an
irrational man, he selected the abstract entity for the discharge of his honest spite," etc. (IX). Victor Radnor, the
Conqueror, represents the "conquering country," spoken
of in the ninth chapter of "Celt and Saxon."

[2] In XXXVI, the author writes of Nesta: "As little as our
native public, had she then any sympathy for the working
of the idea: she wanted throbs, visible aims, the Christian
incarnate."

So I understand the intention of the author in this most abstruse and intricate of his psychological studies. We have to simplify as much as possible, leaving out of account many edifying and some amusing features of the story.[1] The author has pointed the way for us in the recurrence throughout the book of the key-words Optimist and Conqueror. Of these, I have chosen to stand at the head of the chapter the one that has most significance here for the Comic Spirit. There is little laughter in this book. The Comic Spirit has for its text that saying from the Ode,

"Ah, what a fruitless breeder is this heart!"

Its business is to follow the twists of the heart divorced from reason, to follow to the tragic issue the winding paths of self-deception, to prick the iridescent bubbles of illusion. It is an earnest and arduous, to many it may seem a thankless, task. But it is the deliberate chosen labor of the Comic Spirit. And that spirit is sustained in the ardors of this desert-journey by the vision of its goal.[2]

[1] We have, for example, to leave out all mention of the word *punctilio*, which keeps recurring like a droll refrain.
[2] See the end of the chapter on the Comic Philosophy.

CHAPTER VII

THE optimist we have seen to be one variety of sentimentalist. And obviously, in most cases at least, the sentimentalist is strongly tinged with ego. The sentimentalist is so much concerned with his own feelings that, with the best of intentions, he cannot consider the advantage of others. Pity for Emilia, though a prominent factor in the love of Wilfrid Pole, showed itself no practical sentiment, and produced no good results. Victor Radnor's disastrous chivalry in the championing of Nataly and Nesta would have been impossible for one less completely beguiled with sanguine optimism.

As the sentimentalist is almost sure to be an egoist, so the refined egoist is very likely to be affected with sentimentalism.[1] Such an egoist, at any rate, is of more interest to the comic spirit of Meredith; for he exhibits the most subtle

[1] Mr. Curle, in his chapter on Egoism, Sentimentalism, and their Relationship, has something to say on this point.

form of self-deceit. But there are egoists capable
of combining a certain amount of sentimental
self-deception with a practical regard for fact.
They do not allow their sentiment to run away
with them. We cannot imagine in Sir Willoughby
Patterne any such vagueness of aim as that displayed by Wilfrid Pole. He knows what he
wants, and makes straight for it. His sentiments
may be factitious, or misconceived; they are at
least practical. The sentiment is incidental in
his case; he is primarily the egoist.

In itself, egoism is not comic. Self-seeking is
a natural instinct, the motive power of every
organism. Preoccupation with self is a condition of success in a world of competitors. Mere
selfishness may be carried to brutality without
passing through a comic phase.

An egoism is conceivable without the display of
undue vanity or self-esteem. The most obvious
element of the comic in egoism is, to be sure, this
self-conceit quite generally accompanying it.
The ludicrous lies here in the discrepancy between one's actual value and the valuation
assumed by oneself. The humorous writers have
made lavish employment of this, and we have
La-Fooles, Bottoms, Lillyvicks, Micawbers in
plenty. It is hardly necessary to say that Mere-

dith would not engage his comic muse for the
invention of mere coxcombs. The conceit incidental to snob and egoist he does not ignore.
Sir Willoughby Patterne has more body, more
human quality, than many of Meredith's men,
to a large extent because of his touching self-
conceit. But that is not what chiefly interests
Meredith in him. That is not the root of the
comedy.

If the sentimentalist is a product of advanced
civilization, so also is the egoist contemplated by
our comic artist.

The primitive egoist was presumably a frank
and downright brute. Society had not taken
palpable form as an obstruction between the individual and his selfish desire. No convention
or code being recognized but that of his own instincts, the satisfaction of these required no
evasion, no invention of legal periphrasis or
euphemism for the decent veiling of selfishness.
But civilization brings with it society: a set of
ideals governing human intercourse, conventional
standards of the fair and kindly in one's relations
to one's fellows. Manners are softened; men
grow considerate, even altruistic; self is re-
strained, subdued. The golden rule is practised.
Egoism is on the wane. So it appears on the

surface: such is our ideal, and so we like to
represent ourselves. And yet, says the philosopher, egoism flourishes. Competition is lively,
even in our well ordered society. Self-seeking
remains the motive power by which the healthy
organism supports itself. In certain favored
ones, especially, our social system actually cultivates egoism. There are certain personages in
the patriarchal society of England still encour-
aged to hold, with the *grand monarque*, "*L'état
c'est moi.*" And it is not strange they should
give evidence of preoccupation with self.

To be sure, they are highly civilized, keenly
aware of the social conventions, proud of their
own refinement, and anxious to seem models of
altruism. And hence, observes the comic spirit,
arises the masquerade in which I find entertainment. I am always diverted by clever pretence.
I love a mask; and I love to tear it off, exposing
the shamed face behind. It is the difference
that tickles me, the striking discrepancy between
the real and the false face. And I revel in that
moment of surprise and dismay at discovery.
Your modern gentleman is a good actor. He
has been long trained in his part; is letter-perfect,
scrupulous in observance of the *bienséances*,
gracious in bearing, admirable for his bow. His

lines are finished poetry: heroic couplets elegantly turned. I like to trip him up, and send him stumbling into the honest vulgarity of prose. I like to see him stammering and blushing with embarrassment, no longer the accomplished actor of a part. I love to betray the modern gentleman into an exhibition of the primitive egoist.

And the modern gentleman is a thousandfold more open to these shafts than the primitive brute. The latter is presumably concerned only with the satisfaction of physical appetites. The civilized being has discovered a wider realm of finer gratifications. He likes not only success, but the reputation for success. He wishes to win the prize not more on its own account than for the envy and admiration of the disappointed. It is therefore necessary for him not merely to be victor, but to be acclaimed such. He is "a social egoist, fiercely imaginative in whatsoever concerns him." So long as he remains the favored of the gods, he basks in the sunlight of others' admiration, actual or imagined. Let him be conscious of a decline, he feels with equal keenness the chill of others' low regard,—imagining the speech and look of those that have him in view, their scorn or more humiliating pity. Now he grows more concerned for the shadow of honor

than for the substance, labors frantically to re-
tain the shadow, and will even, if necessary,
sacrifice the substance for it. His part becomes
doubly difficult to play. He must observe the
social conventions,—must seem considerate, generous, benevolent; and at the same time he must
seem the conqueror, the enviable and prevailing
one. If he must choose between the two, let him
appear selfish and cruel rather than a failure and
an object of pity. And so he makes himself
doubly pitiable, shut off from human sympathy.

If the egoist be at the same time sentimental,
there is an added spice of comedy. For then he
invests himself in colors still more in contrast
with his actual hue. His worship of self he trans-
lates into the language of sentiment. The desire
for flattery he interprets as the craving for sympathy; and this he attributes to his specially rare
and intense feelings. These feelings he would
make a screen against the perception of unpleasant facts. Nothing is allowed to endanger
the sentimental ideal he has conceived of his own
character. If he be a lover, he is equally anxious
to idealize his lady. He does not want a real
woman, but a puppet of his fancy, fit companion
for his own sentimentalized character. To her
he uses a language carefully chosen to suit her

state of innocence and his own ideal of their relation. And he cultivates with care the æsthetics of that relation, which he regards as intended by providence for his own gratification. Nothing pleases him better than a woman devoted to himself, without his being unduly affected by her. Love he likes to receive and not to give. He does not wish to surrender himself. That would be a loss of the ego.

The social egoist is necessarily, moreover, a snob; because—having regard for the world's opinion of himself—he must have regard for the world's standard of values.

This civilized egoist thus appears a typical representative of the man society knows, comprehending the whole range of pretence and self-deception to which he is liable. And when Meredith wishes to show him to us, he gives him the appropriate family name of Patterne.[1] Sir Willoughby Patterne is no eccentric, nor a man

[1] We have, it would seem, the unfinished portrait of a sentimental egoist in the character of Gilbert Pollingray in "The Gentleman of Fifty and the Damsel of Nineteen." Mr. Pollingray's attitude towards his nephew's love affair reminds one of the attitude of Gen. Ople towards the young lovers in his story; and one guesses at complications somewhat like those into which Sir Willoughby was plunged through his own selfishness. It is a pity this sketch was not completed; for it promises light comedy of the order of "General Ople," and it might have served to extend Meredith's popularity.

marked for ridicule by circumstance or education.
He has the qualities that single one out for admiration.   He is handsome, respectable, well-to-
do, intelligent and cultivated, a man of sense and
wit.   None of us but would gladly accept the
description.   There is no touch of insanity about
him, nothing to suggest the Spanish dreamer.
Providence seems to have left no weak place in
his armor for the shafts of ridicule.   Not in his
outward armor is there a weak spot; but if we
start from within, we shall find sport in plenty.
The twists of the heart, we have read, are the
comedy.   And if there is a man who can follow
Sir Willoughby's twists without acknowledging
some kinship with himself, one must doubt either
his intelligence or his candor.

Sir Willoughby's snobbery is not so much in
evidence as other traits.   He is so well established in the world's estimation that he need not
make pretences.   The snob appears chiefly in his
condescension.   It is not inconceivable that he
might have married Lætitia Dale without being
forced to it to save his face.   He would have
married her as an act of seigneurial condescension, taking her up to his level, but never allowing
her to forget that she had been taken up.   His
attitude towards Vernon Whitford shows the

kind of obtuseness characteristic of the snob. He is unable to see that poor old Vernon, scholar and dependent, is in reality a better man than himself, or he could never have brought himself to make him a present of Clara. Snobbery is sufficiently illustrated in the first chapter. Sir Willoughby is first presented to us in the act of cutting a relation, declining to receive a worthy and heroic man because he was not dressed like a gentleman. If he sent him money privately by way of indemnification, we mark his generosity as hardly more than a sop to his egoism.

We do not wonder at Sir Willoughby's self-conceit when we hear the strain in which Mrs. Jenkinson pronounces his eulogy. He is to his county what Queen Elizabeth was to England, the symbol and embodiment of itself, and he seems to have met with as much adulation from a society admiring itself. He has developed an ideal of himself as *grand seigneur* after the French pattern of the seventeenth century; he would combine in himself the solidity of England with the wit and gallantry of France, the grace of the Restoration cavalier with the sober decency of the modern gentleman. Everyone agrees to accept that ideal of him. When allowed his own way, he shows himself invariably a gracious and

generous sovereign.   But we find that he is indeed
sovereign, with reserves of the tyrant for rebellion.

It is in his relation to women that he betrays
the egoist.   This is characteristic of Meredith's
comic figures.   The comedy is so fine, so much a
matter of character, as not to be observed in
ordinary social intercourse from a distance.   It
is the lady favored with his intimacy that can
read him.   That is why Sir Austin was given a
Lady Blandish though the story does not require
a love affair.   Sir Willoughby has the ill fortune to be read in succession by two intelligent
women.   If we do not count Constantia Durham,
it was Clara Middleton who had the first opportunity to read Sir Willoughby.   Lætitia Dale had
known him from the first, but had not observed
him at close range.   From her cottage on the
borders of his realm, she could only see this prince
of the county as that other poet from his Irish
home beheld the splendid Empress of Britain.

But though Lætitia does not at this time appreciate Sir Willoughby's real character, it shows
itself to us in his attitude towards her.   Sir
Willoughby's fondness for her was but a fondness
for himself.   He loved her for the reflection of
his own splendor.   On his return to England after
his travels, he went to her to find what he most

loved in England. He seized her hand. He asked after her health. "The anxious question permitted him to read deeply in her eyes. He found the man he sought there, squeezed him passionately, and let her go." Lætitia he wished to keep as a sweet feeder to his personal egoism. But she was too humble a person to be chosen for a bride. His social egoism required the selection of some one with qualities to dazzle the world of males.

Such a one he found in Clara Middleton, who had "money and health and beauty, the triune of perfect starriness, which makes all men astronomers." Sir Willoughby, we are informed, had been something of a hunter of women, rejoicing in the exhilaration of the sport, and glad to display trophies won in competition with others. Clara Middleton, as well as Constantia Durham, was snatched from competitors. The inexperienced young creature was easily won by his whirlwind wooing. She was not so easily kept.

She began very early to feel in his courtship something peculiar. There was an unnatural heat in his demand for assurance of affection. His ego had constantly to be fed. He wanted to be sure not only of her heart, but of her soul as well. He wanted her to "reduce herself to

ashes, or incense, or essence, in honor of him,
and so, by love's transmutation, literally be the
man he was." His imagination has long range.
He wishes to pledge her in advance of their marriage never, in case of his death, to marry again.
He is most insistent upon this unpleasant theme.
He attributes his desire to the strength of his
passion, the delicacy of his sentiment. She feels
it to be the unnatural craving of his ego to be
assured absolute possession. The author puts it
in terms of the sordid world. Sir Willoughby
wished to "effect the soul-insurance of his bride,
that he might hold the security of the policy."
And as he cannot bear the thought of her falling
to another after his death, so he requires of a
woman when she comes to him that she shall be
perfectly innocent of men, absolutely spotless
and without history.

This demand for purity is analyzed relentlessly
and with subtle penetration. The author will not
let us forget, beneath a genteel dress, the primitive brute, greedy for absolute possession, and he
indicates the deceits to which women are driven
by this voracity.

"Now, strange and awful though it be to hear,
women perceive this requirement of them in the
spirit of the man; they perceive, too, and it may

be gratefully, that they address their perform-
ances less to the taming of the green and prankish
monsieur of the forest than to the pacification of
a voracious æsthetic gluttony, craving them in-
satiably, through all the tenses, *with shrieks of
the lamentable letter 'I' for their purity*. Whether
they see that it has its foundation in the sensual,
and distinguish the ultra-refined but lineally
great-grandson of the Hoof in this vast and
dainty exacting appetite is uncertain. They
probably do not; the more the damage; for in
the appeasement of the glutton they have to
practise much simulation; they are in their way
losers like their ancient mothers. It is the palpable and material of them still which they are
tempted to flourish wherewith to invite and allay
pursuit: a condition under which the spiritual,
wherein their hope lies, languishes. The capa-
ciously strong in soul among women will ulti-
mately detect an infinite grossness in the demand
for purity infinite, spotless bloom. Earlier or
later they see they have been *victims of the singular
Egoist*, have worn a mask of ignorance to be
named innocent, have turned themselves into
market produce for his delight, and have really
abandoned the commodity in ministering to the
lust for it, suffered themselves to be dragged
ages back in playing upon the fleshly innocence
of happy accident to gratify his jealous greed of
possession, when it should have been their task
to set the soul above the fairest fortune, and the
gift of strength in women beyond ornamental
whiteness. Are they not of a nature warriors,
like men?—men's mates to bear them heroes
instead of puppets? But the *devouring male
Egoist* prefers them as inanimate overwrought
polished pure-metal precious vessels, fresh from
the hands of the artificer, for him to walk away

with hugging, call all his own, drink of, and fill
and drink of, and forget that he stole them."

Clara Middleton, a woman of especially independent spirit, soon realized that her union with
Sir Willoughby involved the surrender of independence. She felt the baser elements in his
over-ardent love. And everywhere—in every
relation—she began to observe the signs of egoism, of selfishness, tyranny and conceit. And
finally he supplies the very title for himself, all
unconscious of its application. After relating a
story about a certain selfish man much like himself, he remarks:

" 'Now there, Clara, there you have the
Egoist. That is the perfect Egoist. . . .
The man was utterly unconscious of giving vent
to the grossest selfishness.'
" 'An Egoist!' said Clara.
" 'Beware of marrying an Egoist, my dear!'
He bowed gallantly; and so blindly fatuous did
he appear to her, that she could hardly believe
him guilty of uttering the words she had heard
from him. . . . Egoist! She beheld him—
unfortunate, self-designated man that he was!—
in his good qualities as well as bad under the
implacable lamp, and his good were drenched in
his first person singular. His generosity roared
of *I* louder than the rest."

When she makes an effort to get released, she
sounds greater depths of egoism. Sir Willoughby

cannot conceive what ails her unless it be jealousy of Lætitia Dale.   Then it is he makes that
declaration, three times pronounced with increas-
ing emphasis, that he could never think of marrying Lætitia Dale.   A beautiful irony this wears
in view of the outcome.   When actually she begs
to be released, giving assurance that it is not
jealousy that moves her, he can no longer shield
himself with this notion; but the ancient egoist
asserts himself, in civilized language, in his refusal to give up the spoil.   The social egoist does
not realize that his bride will make confidants of
his cousin and his female admirer; and that his
one constant devotee will begin from that moment to doubt and grow cold.

Thus begins comic justice to work.   With the
arrival of Horace De Craye, it begins to work
furiously.   Jealousy seizes on Sir Willoughby.
Heretofore he has been free from this passion so
foreign to the complacent and prosperous egoist.
The egoist will not admit so uncomfortable an
inmate to his breast until compelled to it.   When
admitted, it proves close kin to egoism.   "Jealousy of a woman," we read, "is primitive egoism
seeking to refine in a blood gone to savagery
under apprehension of an invasion of rights; it
is in action the tiger threatened by a rifle when

his paw is rigid on quick flesh; he tears the flesh
for rage at the intruder." The egoist wishes to
be ever the one to inflict pain where pain is to be
suffered. It maddens him to think that he is a
dupe, still more to think that the world knows
him for a dupe.

In his efforts to remain the fortunate one, in
fact and in public estimation, Sir Willoughby is
led a merry chase through the bogs of deceit and
humiliation. Wishing to be assured of the affections of one woman, he carries his pathetic case
to Lætitia, lowering his cherished dignity for the
sake of a little sympathy. But she has heard the
other side of the case, and has come to read him
by the light of Clara's lamp. The tears she gives
him are actually tears of pity for herself. Mrs.
Mountstuart Jenkinson represents the gossiping
world; and Sir Willoughby abandons truth to
persuade her that jealousy is what ails Clara.
A vain attempt considering Mrs. Jenkinson's
interview with Clara just afterwards. Ladies
Busshe and Culmer are hard on the scent. Lady
Busshe has dropped the terrible suggestion that
Sir Willoughby might be *twice* jilted. Mrs.
Jenkinson has from the beginning characterized
Clara as a "rogue." "The breath of the world,
the world's view of him, was partly his vital

breath, his view of himself." Some step is
urgently required by which he may set himself
right in the eyes of the world.

Sir Willoughby determines to transfer his
affections to Lætitia. That is not so miracu-
lous a feat as it might seem. The social egoist
must above all maintain the appearance of success. No mere desirable creature must be allowed
to weigh in the scales against oneself. Clara
Middleton cannot be had. It must not seem
that he was cast off by her. She must be the
jilted one. It might be made to appear that he
preferred Lætitia. Though poor and faded, she
has brains. She is certainly more sympathetic.
An imagination under pressure could be brought
to dress her in some of the colors of beauty.

Sir Willoughby had once contemplated be-
stowing Lætitia upon his cousin Vernon. At
that time, he had come to regard her as not too
dear to be yielded up. It was now Clara that he
would toss to Vernon. He was not unwilling
that she should bear the shame of being dis-
carded. He imagined the gossip of the world,
not unflattering to the *grand seigneur:* "And he
handed her to his cousin and secretary, Vernon
Whitford, who opened his mouth and shut his
eyes." Anything so that she may not fall to

his rival De Craye. He did not realize that his
actual rival was "poor old Vernon."

Humiliations are in store for him. When he
stoops to ask the hand of the woman he does
not want, he finds to his dismay that she no
longer wants him. He still persecutes his fiancée,
and dares to talk of fidelity! The elements are
against him: his proposal to Lætitia was overheard. A useless lie covers him with shame while
one person after another discovers a knowledge
of the truth. He conducts a frantic campaign of
mystification for the benefit of the gossips. At
last he accomplishes his desire. His intrepid
generalship triumphs. But what a barren victory! The woman he loves he must give up to
the man she really loves. He wins for himself a
faded and disillusioned bride, who insists on telling him his faults to his face, and, what is worse,
in the presence of his admiring family. The one
person whom he trusted to remain faithful in
admiration has discovered his real character. It
may be the countryside will put upon these events
a construction favorable to his vanity. He cannot expect longer in his home that luxury of
flattered self-esteem.

The career of the egoist carries on its face its
own sufficient moral. This unsocial being for-

feits the chief benefits of society: human sympathy, the amenities of equal intercourse, the give and take of mutual consideration and respect. The sweet kernel he throws away to save the fruitless shell. In the attempt to preserve his dignity he has made himself ridiculous and despicable. He has merely succeeded in exhibiting, for the delectation of the comic spirit, a striking contrast between the primitive man he is and the social being he would appear.

CHAPTER VIII

THE ROMANTIC EPICURE

SIR WILLOUGHBY was something of a sentimentalist. But he was also a most sensible,
hard-headed Englishman, as he would have said
himself; and sentiment was decidedly subordinate to the social egoism that controlled him.
Wilfrid Pole showed himself an egoist in his
irresponsible indulgence in sentiment. But he
was not a confirmed egoist who considered only
himself; and sentimentality was the prevailing
character in him. In the case of Lord Fleetwood, male protagonist of the "Amazing Marriage," both characters are so marked and so
essential to the plot, it requires a constant reference to them both to explain his fantastic behavior. Fleetwood was not, however, so much
of a social egoist as Sir Willoughby, and was not
driven to such desperate ludicrous shifts to
defend his vanity. It is interesting to watch the
manœuvres of his personal ego in the effort to
justify itself and shun the feeling of compunc-

tion! And without these manœuvres, we cannot understand how he was able to treat his wife so cruelly. But more important it is to understand why he should have *wished* to treat her so, what was the original source of his vagary. The real key to his character is the special variety of sentimentalism to which he was subject. His egoism served merely to aid and abet him in his unnatural craving for romance. This romantic epicurism was to some extent exemplified by Wilfrid Pole; but in the person of Fleetwood, Meredith has made a more extended, more interesting and significant study of the type. And a view of this sentimental egoist will carry us somewhat farther in our interpretation of Meredith's comic spirit.

The Earl of Fleetwood was, in the first place, the wealthiest nobleman of England. The author makes it plain enough what connection the young man's great wealth and high rank have with his character. This book should be read by the light of Meredith's opinions expressed in the "Empty Purse." In that singular poem, he traces the inevitable effect on character of the inheritance of great wealth, and condemns the

> "grandmotherly laws
> Giving rivers of gold to our young,

In the days of their hungers impure;
To furnish them beak and claws,
And make them a banquet's lure."

So in the novel we have unmistakable evidence
of Meredith's socialistic view.[1]   One might suppose the "Amazing Marriage" to be intended,
like the "Empty Purse," for a piece of Radical
propaganda.   Only Meredith, when he represents
human nature full length, offers more than argument for a social principle.   Though an extreme
and exceptional case, the Earl of Fleetwood
exemplifies universal human tendencies easily
fostered by circumstance.   His pride and arro-
gance, his ambition to be leader of men, have
been allowed to grow to extravagance, and are
given room to exhibit themselves in flaring eccen-
tricity of act.   His tyranny and caprice are but
the tyranny and caprice of a child, not disciplined,
as in others, by competition and correction.

His caprice may, further, be traced to the
Welsh blood upon which so much stress is laid.
And we may associate with his Celtic origin his
sort of romantic sentimentalism.   The Earl of
Fleetwood did not class himself with others of
his rank,—material-minded, frank lovers of sport
and sensual pleasure, brainless and without im-

[1] See especially XXVI, XXVIII, and compare XLIV.

agination. He prided himself on his originality, on his romantic love of solitude, his mystical sensibility, and his cultivation of the poetry of sentiment. Though not by nature a dreamer, he had so much of the Celt that he dreamed of the luxury of being one; and he was generous in admiration of Lord Feltre, the religious mystic, as well as of Gower Woodseer, the natural philosopher.

Fleetwood was keenly sensitive to the charm of women; and of women he was a discriminating admirer. He could grow heated in debate with Woodseer over the latter's impressionistic phrases in description of Carinthia. He was an amateur in sentiment, a connoisseur of the sensations produced by feminine personality. Carinthia caught him through "his passion for the wondrous in the look of a woman's face, the new morning of the idea of women in the look, and the peep into imaginary novel character." The very sufferings of women could furnish music to him. He had the libertine's pleasure in the quivers of feeling observed in his victim. He enjoyed the sensations of Madge while she watched the prize-fight in which her lover was engaged. "She had the tone of the woman who can be screwed to witness a spill of blood, peculiarly catching to hear—a

tone of every string in them snapped except the
silver string.   Catching to hear?   It is worth a
stretching of them on the rack to hear that
low buzz-hum of the inner breast. . . . By
heaven! we have them at their best when they
sing that note."   The æsthetic gluttony of the
male is in Fleetwood refined to the taste of an
imaginative epicure.   We read the following record of sensations in relation to his wife:

"The respect enforced by her attitude awak-
ened in him his inherited keen relish for our inter-
sexual strife and the indubitable victory of the
stronger, with the prospect of slavish charms,
marrowy spoil.   Or perhaps, preferably, a sullen
submission, reluctant charms; far more marrowy.
Or who can say?—the creature is a rocket of the
shot into a fiery garland of stars; she may per-
sonate any new marvel, be an unimagined terror,
an overwhelming bewitchment: for she carries
the unexpected in her bosom."

It is the last sentence that suggests the Celtic
imagination.   Fleetwood was a Celt among
Saxons in his craving for romance, for magic,
the sense of the super-terrestrial in a maiden's
love.

"The love they versify, and strum on guitars,
and go crazy over, and end by roaring at as the
delusion; this common bloom of the ripeness of
the season; this would never have utterly cap-
tured a sceptic, to vanquish him in his mastery,

snare him in her surrender. It must have been
the veritable passion: a flame kept alive by
vestal ministrants in the yew-wood of the forest
of Old Romance; planted only in the breasts of
very favourite maidens. Love had eyes, love
had a voice that night,—love was the explicable
magic lifting terrestrial to seraphic.''

Fleetwood was the sentimentalist not because
of his poetic sensibility, his appetite for romance;
but because he was so generally unable to recognize true romance when he found it, because his
poetic sensibility was too easily offended by the
wholesome and the natural. His wife "he had
accused as the creature destroying Romance. Was
it gold in place of gilding, absolute upper human
life that she proposed instead of delirious brillian-
cies, drunken gallops, poison-syrups,—puffs of a
young man's vapours?" Lord Fleetwood is a
deluded and comic figure because he will build
for himself, out of gaseous bubbles of desire, an
iridescent structure that cannot stand a breath
of the wind of truth; and all the while the
veritable temple of romance stands before him
unrecognized as such because its stones are
weather-stained in real sunlight. He reverses the
error of Don Quixote, who saw giants in wind-
mills, armies in a flock of sheep. The Spaniard
saw more than there was in the object. Fleet-

wood sees less. In that, his case is more pathetic than the Spaniard's, who at least idealized whatever he saw. And his case is more pathetic, too, because he is not altogether insane. He is forever having glimpses of the truth; and in the end, he is obliged to forego the poetry of his life when he at last with certainty identifies it.

None of Meredith's heroines more unmistakably stands for his ideal than Carinthia. She has the simplicity of nature. Her education has kept her innocent of conventionhand free from affectation. She gives her and or her heart with perfect naïveté. Until the facts enlighten her, she trusts mankind. Neglect and cruelty she bears with quiet courage, but without meekness. She will resign herself to necessity; but she maintains her rights. She is the perfect mother, concerned above all for the welfare of her offspring. A loyal and devoted sister, she is capable of being a warm and affectionate wife. She does not harbor personal grudge against the man that wrongs her; but once taught to despise him, she cannot again admit him to the intimacy of her soul. She has a spirit of perfect natural beauty. She sees the world as it is, with clear and unrefracted vision; but she looks upon it from a noble heart, loving it and dwelling upon

the noble in it. She discovers the beautiful in
character by affinity. She is an idealist in her
appreciation of human beings; but she will not
maintain her ideal of a person in the face of con-
tradicting evidence. She is not afraid of the
commonplace, but she never touches the dull or
the vulgar. Everything she does and says is rare
in a world of tawdriness. She has, morally and
physically, the fresh loveliness and distinction of
a natural object, of virgin landscape or a wild
flower. She is the very incarnation of essential
romance.

And this was instinctively discerned by Fleetwood on the night when he met her and offered
her his hand. We need not suppose that the
only motive to this act was disappointed love or
wounded vanity. Not every woman would have
served for solace to his amorous distress over the
loss of Henrietta. In the ball-room full of the
hothouse blooms of society, he felt the charm of
this mountain girl, the appeal of true romance.
Yet, while acting in accordance with his higher
instincts, he had acted upon impulse; and his
faith was naturally weak. Immediately he re-
gretted the whim that bound him to a poor
uncultivated girl of no social standing. But the
first law of his pride forbade the violation of his

word of honor; and he did not fail to keep it in
this instance. Fleetwood did not know that his
bride had been kept ignorant of his reluctance to
marry her; and this initial misunderstanding
made him ready to misinterpret every point in
her behavior. Her addressing him as "my husband" seemed like the flaunting of her conquest.
Even her pluck in witnessing the prize-fight he
twisted to her discredit. It was to be expected
that her father's daughter would show sporting
blood. Her touching simplicity in the scene
when he left her at the inn of the creaking sign
could not fail to make its impression; but he
was not yet ready to be reconciled to this ridiculous marriage. His midnight visit to his wife
almost converted him. He found in her then
a distinctive personal charm that satisfied his
romantic demand. But there was a lively devil
in him to suggest another order of romance.
His self-love could not support with patience the
notion that his Henrietta should love the man
she had married. And his devil kept proposing
a trial. It would be a comfort to the wounded
egoist in him to prove her unworthy of his love.

Then came the Whitechapel business; and the
wealthiest nobleman of England had the humiliation of learning that his wife had been living in a

shop in that dreadful quarter, and was creating
huge entertainment in society gossip as Lord
Fleetwood's Whitechapel Countess. As if this
were not enough, there followed the scene in the
park in which the Earl of Fleetwood found himself actually defended from attack by a woman
wielding a stick, and that woman recognized as
his own Countess. It would take sturdy romance
to survive such disillusioning circumstances.

When the birth of his child promised to wake
nature in the man, the defensive instincts of the
egoist came forward to make him his wife's
enemy. He could not but admit her admirable
qualities. But he was obliged to find excuse for
his own despicable conduct. He must manage
to put the blame on another. "She was thrust
away because she had offended; still more because he had offended. She bore the blame for
forcing him to an examination of his conduct at
this point and that, where an ancestral savage in
his lineaments cocked a strange eye." He managed to transfer the blame to Carinthia by an
unfavorable comparison of her with the Henrietta she was expected to supply the place of.
"He had now to vindicate himself by extinguish-
ing her under the load of her own unwomanliness:
she was like sun-dried linen matched beside ori-

ental silk: she was rough, crisp, unyielding.
That was now the capital charge." At this point,
the necessities of self-esteem fortified him in his
false taste in women. The more he had to admire
her, the more his pride rebelled. It was still
worse after her act of cool-blooded heroism in
the incident of the mad dog and the bitten child.
Unable to support the thought of her actual
superiority, the husband falls back upon the
specious advantages of his wealth and station;
and summons likewise his notion of himself as a
complex, highly civilized man, not easily to be
accounted for, and not to be held accountable.[1]
In the "Empty Purse," we read of the wealthy
young profligate who derived similar comfort
from his social advantage.

> "——some one said
> (Or was it the thought into hearing grew?)
> *Not thou as commoner men!*
> Thy stature puffed and it swayed,
> It stiffened to royal-erect;
> A brassy trumpet brayed;
> A whirling seized thy head;
> The vision of beauty was flecked."

Thus Fleetwood summoned a brassy trumpet to
drown the voice of nature; and his vision of
beauty was flecked.

[1] So Victor Radnor comes to think of himself: "I'm not
to be questioned like other men."

At last the true charm and rareness of Carinthia grows upon him till he can no longer hold out against her. He comes to realize that his bride has never really been wooed. He spends a night at the inn with the terrible creaking sign; and his own fastidious sense teaches him how much she has had to suffer. But now that he is converted to the way of duty and happiness combined, he lacks courage to make full confession and abasement. He does indeed speak "arterial words," even in the presence of Carin's brother; but his pride forbids that complete exposure of past meanness that "shows our fellows that the slough is cast." There is no feeling left in Carinthia to draw her back to him save pity. And even pity gives way before Henrietta's revelation of his dastard course. Carin departs with her brother on the Spanish expedition in the cause of freedom. Fleetwood enters a monastery, and dies of his austerities under religious rule.

In the view of the author, this conclusion must have had the same moral significance as suicide, and the same explanation as the self-murder of Purcell Barrett, that earlier study of the discouraged sentimentalist. The pseudo-mysticism, the æsthetic epicurism of Fleetwood found its

appeal in the symbolism and ritualism of the
Church. For the pricks of conscience and the
throbs of a wounded pride, his friend Lord Feltre
offered the consolatory salves of religion. The
choice of Feltre's religion in place of Woodseer's
philosophy had the advantage of absolving the
Earl from true self-examination, and from all the
servile task of mending a broken life. He was
naturally superstitious, inclined even to attribute
his misfortunes to an evil star, a peculiar fatalism
that controlled his destiny. Or he agreed with
Dame Gossip in referring his own acts to mystery, to the irony of life. It relieved him of the
onerous burdens of self-analysis and reform. It
was the troubles of sex that disturbed his high
serenity; and, providentially for him, it was
precisely woman, Venus, nature, that the Church
distinguished as its peculiar enemy. "The two
sexes created to devour one another must abjure
their sex before they gain 'The Peace,' as Feltre
says, impressively." Fleetwood's immediate duty
was communication with his wife. But his pride
would not permit the writing of what must be
written to reestablish their relations.

"He remembered Gower Woodseer's having
warned him he would finish his career as a monk.
Not, like Feltre, an oily convert, but under the

hood, yes, and extracting a chartreuse from his
ramble through woods richer far than the philosopher's milk of Mother Nature's bosom.   There
flamed the burning signal of release from his tor-
ments; there his absolving refuge, instead of his
writing fruitless, intricate, impossible stuff to a
woman.   The letter was renounced and shredded:
the dedicated ascetic contemplated a hooded shape,
washed of every earthly fleck.   It proved how men
may by grip squeeze raptures out of pain."

The religious retirement of Fleetwood was, like
the suicide of Purcell Barrett, a sentimental
abandonment of the truth, a cowardly surrender; and it is evidence of a malady prevalent
among the most highly developed, the over-
refined, those refined to the breaking point.   This
sentimentalism is, in fact, a symptom of deca-
dence.   There was little of the decadent about
Wilfrid Pole.   In the end, he grew into something
more than a philanderer; and we find him, in
"Vittoria," serving his god of love with the
tenacity that comes of faith.   He was no mere
amorous dilettante.   Still less of the decadent
was there about Sir Willoughby Patterne.   His
was at least a healthy egoism.   Not so Fleetwood's.   In this combination with perverse romantic sentimentalism, egoism itself becomes
decadent, and the root of life turns poisonous
and serves life's enemy.

Snobbery, sentimentalism, egoism,—these are the three comic traits which Meredith finds to be most characteristic of our half-refined society. They all run together in this last of Meredith's figures; and he illustrates their essential kinship most strikingly perhaps of all Meredith's characters,—especially the close kinship of sentimentalism and egoism, those two cunning actors of many parts. In this final study, our author shows how cleverly they play together, how subtly they disguise themselves from the perception of the man whose soul is their stage. The sentimentalist proves a self-indulgent egoist. The modern egoist is a sentimental self-deceiver, one who plays, without knowing it, the wolf in sheep's clothing.

CHAPTER IX

ALL Meredith's comic figures are studies in civilization unperfected. Especially in the later novels, we meet with the contrast or the struggle between the civilized and the uncivilized elements in human character. The egoist is the selfish primitive who has extended his desires to include a wide range of social gratifications; the complex uncivilized man talking the dialect of the complex civilized. The sentimentalist regards himself as in the van of spiritual progress, when he is really using the ideals of civilization as an excuse for spiritual laziness and deceit. This front rank of marching society is where the observer will find those comic contrasts most provocative of thoughtful laughter. Here are the greatest pretensions to refinement, and here therefore its lack is most striking when discovered. Here is found the greatest refinement in fact, and the most striking contrast, accordingly, with the coexisting primitive.

The contrast is comic. The results are sometimes amusing, sometimes pathetic, sometimes
tragic; as we have seen in Meredith's novels.
Of Victor and Nataly Radnor, it might be said,
as of Alvan and Clothilde, that "the comic in
their natures led by interplay to the tragic issue."
The more serious the characters involved, the
more likely it is that a notable weakness will lead
to a tragic outcome. In the case of both Victor
Radnor and Doctor Alvan, it may well be said,
in view of their titanic power,

> "Now all labour
> Mars what it does; yea, very force entangles
> Itself with strength."

They were men whom the author could designate, without irony, as conquerors. They were
actually men of genius and prevailing charm.
Alvan stands for the political leader whom many
regarded as one of the two greatest men in his
Europe. And yet their strength was their undoing. The machine, being not well balanced,
was thrown out of order, and tore itself to pieces
with its own violence.

The earlier of these two studies we consider
last of all. The "Tragic Comedians" is not a
work of fiction, but a faithful rendering of true
history, with only such comments and minor

inventions of the novelist as were necessary to
illuminate and interpret the strange incidents.[1]
Meredith has taken some pains to follow point
for point the narrative of the surviving actor in
this drama. He wished, so to speak, to demon-
strate his comic method by applying it to an
actual and notorious series of events ending in
catastrophe. He has, in his novels, made various efforts to present human nature in a critical
light; exerting himself in particular to trace in
character the comic traits that result in unheroic,
sometimes in tragic, action. He has tried to
laugh people out of the notion that their acts
are controlled by things outside themselves: by
fate, fortune, luck, providence, or any agency
unconnected with their own character. He has

[1] Dr. Alvan = Ferdinand Lassalle; Clothilde von Rüdi-
ger = Helene von Dönniges, later von Racowitza, and then
Countess Schewitsch; Prince Marko = Yanko von Racowitza. See Hammerton, pp. 250–255. An account of the
history from her own point of view is given by the lady
(von Racowitza) in "Meine Beziehungen zu Ferdinand
Lassalle," Breslau, 1879, etc. This is Meredith's main authority. The account has been somewhat amplified by
Frau von Schewitsch in her reminiscences entitled "Von
Anderen und mir," Berlin, 1910 (fourth edition). There
is an English translation of this. Other books and articles
on the story are referred to in Lane's bibliography. Lassalle is represented by Leo Gutmann in Spielhagen's novel
"In Reih' und Glied"; but there is no resemblance in the
treatment, and not much resemblance in the incidents, to
the "Tragic Comedians." Israel Zangwill has also treated
the incidents of this tragedy in a story called "The Saviour
of the People" in his "Dreamers of the Ghetto."

shown men belying themselves, deceiving themselves, putting off responsibility for their acts,
trying to lay on the irony or mystery of things
what they are too delicate or sensitive to trace
to their own deceitful hearts. He is now struck
with a strange fantastic history from real life,
easy to seize upon as illustration of the irony of
fate, of the arbitrary ways of the gods. And he
undertakes to interpret it in the light of the
comic spirit, by reference to human motives,
common and natural though so remarkably displayed. The undertaking is the more interesting
because of the exceptional character of the leading actor. He is superhuman in strength and
complexity. But his weakness is human, and
the woven elements of character; and they serve
to illustrate the nature of common men. And if
fate so fantastic as this may be referred to character, need there be a question of it in the pedes-
trian comedy of ordinary men?

Doctor Alvan was a man of superabundant
energies, of warm and active imagination, of
boundless self-confidence. He had been used to
success; everybody succumbed to his personal
charm. But he was a Jew, a revolutionary, a
free-liver, with a history that might easily be
represented in black colors; and when, at middle

age, he undertook to marry a Christian girl, from a noble family of Philistines, he did not fully reckon the difficulties. Accustomed to the admiration and friendship of those about him, he did not realize the world's view of him. He thought himself indomitable, a Titan, a sungod; and his sanguine temperament touched with its rose hues the actual circumstances of the case. It was impossible for him to conceive failure in relation to himself.

Now Doctor Alvan, the social insurgent, is not the less a creation of civilized society, and he wishes to win his bride according to the rules of the game, and to achieve a victory over prejudice by sheer personal ascendancy. When Clothilde, frightened at the prospect of the struggle with her family, comes to his hotel to place herself in his hands, he refuses to take advantage of the opportunity to marry her without the consent of her parents. He wishes to astonish them with the civilized character of this Jewish demagogue, who, when he might have their daughter by right of capture, fails not to pay every respect to their legal and natural claims. The author emphasizes the comic paradox in Alvan's procedure here. "He was a wild man, cased in the knowledge of jurisprudence, and wishing to enter

the ranks of the soberly blissful." And so at the
interview with Clothilde's mother in the neutral
drawing-room, in spite of the evident desire of
Clothilde to the contrary, and the mute warning
she tries to convey to him, he insists on yielding
her for the present in order to have her back
again with the more honor.

This is the great comic scene of the book,
though there is little laughter in it. Alvan was
committing an act of magnanimous folly. He
had thoroughly gauged the character of his lady;
knew her to be impulsive, shifty, weak as water.
Indeed he was pleased to think, in all stages of
their love-making, that what character she possessed was given her by himself. He was the
magnetic pole and she the compass always pointing towards him. Her very soul was a gift. "I
give her a soul! I am the wine, and she the
crystal cup." And yet, fully aware of the weakness of his lady, he would give her up to the
enemy, confident in his power to win her back
again. In the lady's account, so closely followed
by Meredith, there is no attempt to read the
character of the lover. The scene is related only
in its dramatic and sentimental aspects, without
consideration for character, which is everywhere
to this lady a riddle she does not take the trouble

to solve.   But Meredith, with an occasional turn
of expression, brings out the ludicrousness of
Alvan's behavior, and makes Clothilde feel it
herself.   To the brutalities of Clothilde's mother
Alvan replied with unruffled politeness, aglow
with his own moral grandeur in the act.   The
young lady, conscious of her want of courage,
began to reproach him in her heart, and she
watched him with critical, unsympathetic eye.
"He kissed cold lips, he squeezed an inanimate
hand.   The horribly empty sublimity of his behavior appeared to her in her mother's contemp-
tuous face."   "He smiled insufferably.   He was
bent on winning a parent-blessed bride, a lady
handed to him instead of taken, one of the world's
polished silver vessels."   The primitive man has
adopted the pride of the civilized member of
society; he shows himself the social egoist.   He
makes the same demand as Sir Willoughby for
spotless "ornamental whiteness."   Like Sir Willoughby, he imagines what the world will say,
putting into the mouth of personified society a
scroll with words on it: "Alvan's wife was honor-
ably won, as became the wife of a Doctor of Law,
from the bosom of her family, when he could have
had her in the old lawless fashion, for a call to a
coachman!   Alvan, the republican, is eminently

a citizen. Consider his past life by that test of his character." And so he takes on the somewhat ludicrous appearance of a tamed monster. "He who had many times defied the world in hot rebellion, had become, through his desire to cherish a respectable passion, if not exactly slavish to it, subservient, as we see royal personages, that are happy to be on bowing terms with a multitude bowing lower."

In spite of the folly of Alvan's course in view of the acknowledged weakness of Clothilde and the confirmed opposition of her family, in spite of the fatuous vanity that prompted his action, there was yet an aspect of chivalry about it. It was the act of a civilized being possessed of consideration for the claims of others. But as soon as he met with tough resistance, as soon as he experienced the results of Clothilde's weakness, and felt the strength it gave to his enemies, the primitive came again to the surface. "Dignity was cast off; he came out naked." The comic spirit chuckles grimly at the unmasking of the primitive.

"She had roused the sportman's passion as well as the man's; he meant to hunt her down, and was not more scrupulous than our ancient hunters, who hunted for a meal and hunted to kill, with none of the later hesitations as to circumventing, trapping, snaring by devices, and the preservation

of the animal's coat spotless.   Let her be lured from
her home, and if reluctant, disgraced, that she
may be dependent utterly on the man stooping
to pick her up!   He was equal to the projecting
of a scheme socially infamous, with such fanatical
intensity did the thought of losing the woman
harass him, and the torrent of his passion burst
restraint to get to her to enfold her—*this in the
same hour of the original wild monster's persistent
and sober exposition of the texts of the law with the
voice of a cultivated modern gentleman;* and, let it
be said, with a modern gentleman's design to wed
a wife in honour.''

The italicized words remind us that the "Tragic
Comedians" was published the year following
the "Egoist." Alvan is in a very different class
from Sir Willoughby. He is a more volcanic,
more fearfully elemental spirit. He is a splendid
heroic figure, treated by the author with sympathy and respect. But he shows the same
picture of the uncivilized masquerading as the
civilized, unconscious of the mask; and we distinguish in him, as well as in Sir Willoughby,
"the ultra-refined but lineally great-grandson of
the Hoof." When at last his friend brings word
of Clothilde's repudiation of him, he becomes a
raging beast. He who had heretofore refused
all provocation to the duel, deeming it wasteful,
immoral, inconclusive, unreasonable, sends to
Clothilde's father a challenge to mortal combat,—

become like any creature without reason; and
he launches at his own beloved that blackening
epithet whose stain can never be removed.

Alvan was a perfect shot; and when the great
man fell before the bullet of Prince Marko, the
inexperienced weakling, fighting on account of a
shallow girl, it might seem the capricious whim
and irony of chance.   But he that commits himself to this senseless ordeal must not complain.
It was an irony of character that we are asked to
take account of.

This tragic comedian it is impossible to fit with
neatness into any one of the categories we have
distinguished.   His character is too complex for
that.   He bears perhaps the closest relation to
the sentimental optimist; for it was a sanguine
self-confidence like that of Victor Radnor that
provoked his fate.   One can discern also a kinship to Sir Willoughby; and there is something
like sublimated snobbery in his desire to win a
bride in the fashion prescribed by good society.
But there are still other factors, of the high and
low in character, that complicate the reckoning;
and it is the general contrast of the high and low
in him that impresses the reader, and gives him a
specially typical significance.   The comic action
and the tragic fate of this conqueror were the

result of an ill-assorted or unevenly developed character. It was a "mass of humanity, profusely mixed of good and evil, of generous ire and mutinous, of the passion for the future of mankind and vanity of person, magnanimity and sensualism, high judgment, reckless indiscipline, chivalry, savagery, solidity, fragmentariness." Alvan represents a stage in the civilizing process. He is a type of the giant race growing into spiritual manhood, but overgrown, clumsy, ill-controlled. This body was an easy prey to the forces of dissolution. "The two men composing it, the untamed and the candidate for citizenship, in mutual dissension pulled it down. . . . A stormy blood made wreck of a splendid intelligence." Alvan interests Meredith because he suffered the tragedy of a noble and complex man. He was a man devoted to the cause of humanity. Though a social insurgent by reason of his race and political principle, he represents the best of his time in education and aspiration.[1] He stands in the front rank of civilized beings, and he stands preeminent there for stature and strength. But the lower elements of his nature wrecked him. It is like the tragedy of mankind itself. Only, man-

[1] Of course what is said of Alvan does not necessarily apply to his model Lassalle.

kind is immortal; and many such tragedies and
comedies are but incidents in the process by which
the race as a whole becomes less and less subject
to the shafts of the comic spirit.[1]

[1] I regret that the plan of my chapter makes it impossible to dwell upon the fine comic portrayal of the character
of Clothilde. She is in some ways as interesting as Alvan;
and she might, as Meredith suggests, be made the subject
of a comedy in the school of Menander. She is a notable
study in a kind of sentimental self-deception.

CHAPTER X

FIVE of Meredith's stories we have left out of account.[1] In these, the comic element is so subordinate or incidental that I call them, by reference to Meredith's prevailing theme, diversions. They include some of his most famous novels; but they fall somewhat outside the main current of his production, and are not so characteristic of their author as those we have been considering.

The most commonplace of Meredith's novels is "Diana of the Crossways." Most commonplace because least Meredithian. And therefore

---

[1] Six, if we include "Vittoria." For our present study, this sequel to "Sandra Belloni" is interesting mainly for the continuation of Wilfrid's indecision in his relations to women. I have made reference elsewhere in footnotes to the fragmentary novels, "Celt and Saxon" and "The Gentleman of Fifty and the Damsel of Nineteen." These are full of humor, and they promise true comedy. But as Meredithian comedy resides chiefly in the main idea of the story, we cannot more than guess at its nature in these two books.

most popular with the general public not prepared
for the novelty of Meredith's method.

I do not mean to say that "Diana" is not an
interesting story, a good novel as good novels go,
and, in point of style and detail, sharing the
peculiar splendor of Meredith's other work.   But
in general conception and design, it is almost an
ordinary novel.   There is a divorce suit, an elope-
ment projected, strong temptation of a married
woman and grave suspense; and the fortunes of
the heroine are followed out sympathetically from
her first appearance in society to her ultimate
sensible marriage.   It savors of George Eliot or
even Mrs. Humphry Ward.   A woman of large
energies, of generous and aspiring soul, Diana
Merion aims throughout her career to secure the
freest play for her faculties.   She always means
the best, but she is subject to human weakness.
On her character Meredith has one of his most
beautiful aphorisms: "The light of every soul
burns upward.   Of course, most of them are
candles in the wind.   Let us allow for atmos-
pheric disturbance."   Mr. Trevelyan has pointed
out that the central theme of Meredith's novels is
"the growth of the undesirable young, through
suffering, to spiritual manhood," "the sufferings
by which callow youth wins wisdom and strength,

if the victim is not broken to pieces in the process of the Ordeal." [1] In this respect, "Diana" is a typical book of Meredith's. But this is likewise the predominant theme of George Eliot. George Eliot might have conceived the moral epigram gathered by Diana from the experiences of herself and her friend: "There is nothing the body suffers that the soul may not profit by."

The person whom Meredith might have chosen to treat as comic is Percy Dacier. And there is indeed a hint in him of Wilfrid Pole and Sir Willoughby Patterne. The "frosty Cupid," who was constantly seeking to break through Diana's just reserves, but whose fragile love could bear so little, suggests the philanderer who was tossed to and fro between Sandra and Lady Charlotte. And when the author compares the not impeccable character of Diana, "a growing soul," with that of the "true heroine of romance," we are reminded of the analysis of Sir Willoughby's demand for feminine purity. Diana "was not one whose purity was carved in marble for the assurance to an Englishman that his possession

[1] George Macaulay Trevelyan, "The Poetry and Philosophy of George Meredith," pp. 132, 119. This book contains perhaps the best that has been written about Meredith.

of the changeless thing defies time and his fellows, is the pillar of his home and universally enviable." This is the nearest Meredith comes in "Diana" to the comic treatment that so distinguishes his other books.

Now the sense of the comic is a variety of imagination, not unrelated to poetic fancy, aswe observe in Charles Lamb and Lauremce Sterne. And it is precisely imagination that "Diana" lacks, if we are to compare it with any other story of Meredith. It is a palin narrative of ordinary people, with no touch of the rare to put out the ordinary reader. We feel, as in reading Mrs. Ward's novels ain the school of "Diana," that we are moving in good society. among people of wit and social importance. And we are pleased to feel they are people much like ourselves. Taine would perhaps recognize in this novel one of the regular English school of moral and realistic stories so far removed from the large imagination "that creates and transmutes." [1]

Meredith's later novels, all taken together,

---

[1] In his "History of English Literature," Book IV, chap. I, iv, Taine writes of the English novel: "Réaliste et moral, voila ses deux traits. Ils sont a cents lieues de la grande imagination qui crée ou transforme, telle qu'elle apparut à la Renaissance ou au dix-septième siècle, dans les ages héroïques ou nobles. Ils renoncent a l'invention libre; ils s'astreignent a l'exactitude scrupuleuse." Etc.

constitute a plea for the better understanding of women. If "Diana" has coherent design, it must be found in this theme. A sort of footnote to "Diana" is the little comedy of "Lord Ormont and his Aminta." Lord Ormont is a variant, or slight preliminary sketch, of Lord Fleetwood, quite as subject as he, or Warwick, or Dacier, to a shallow conventional and selfish view of women. He is the ghost of a comic figure: the sulky Achilles, or grown-up child, whose vanity being hurt, he declares he will not play. The conclusion is comic like the end of a fable. By the time he has got ready to acknowledge Lady Ormont, she has transferred her affections to another and better man. You hear the common-sense of our fathers reciting words fraught with the comic experience of the ages:

> "He who will not when he may,
> When he will, he shall have Nay."

"Beauchamp's Career" is somewhat similar to "Diana" in point of construction and theme, though much more distinguished as a work of imagination. It is, like " Diana," the chronicle of one who made the best of circumstances, and tried to find the better way. Of pronounced comedy there is none save that found in the relations of

Nevil to his uncle, especially in the affair of Dr.
Shrapnel.   This is too intense in the strain upon
one's feelings to be amusing in the ordinary way.
I can remember no series of chapters in fiction in
which the suspense is more enthralling than those
in which we are in doubt whether Romfrey will
apologize to Dr. Shrapnel for thrashing him.   But
as one considers the anomalous character of
Nevil's figure in his aristocratic environment, the
strong contrast of his views with those of his
uncle, the conflict of the two stubborn wills, and
their contest of wits, one comes to feel a pervading
comedy in the general situation.   Of course, our
sympathies are with Nevil, and the comic figure
is the anachronistic uncle, "a mediæval gentleman
with the docile notions of the twelfth century,
complacently driving them to grass and wattling
them in the nineteenth."   But the comic lies
here in situation, or composition, rather than in
individual characters;   it is the struggle of the
two, and of the groups they centre, that makes
the element of comedy in the book.

Nevil did not succeed in his ambition.   He was
not allowed to serve his country as a law-maker.
The results he achieved in private and public
life were insignificant.   But he was not the one
to blame.   Consider the obstacles.   Consider his

stolid Philistine opponent. His want of success,
says the author, "does not forbid him to be ranked
as one of the most distinguishing of her children
of the day he lived in. Blame the victrix if you
think he should have been livelier." Perhaps we
should regard as the comic butt of this story not
so much Everard Romfrey as the stupid England
of which he and his confederates are but types.
The book is rather a satire on conservatism than
a panegyric of radicalism. This is characteristic
of Meredith. Another author would have had
his hero overcome all obstacles, and triumph.
Meredith, controlled by the comic spirit, displays
the well-nigh hopeless struggle of a highminded
modern gentleman with lingering feudal traditions. Could Meredith but have lived to record
the present struggle in England, what a comedy
we might have!

There remain to consider "Rhoda Fleming"
and the "Tale of Chloe."

"Rhoda Fleming" is distinctly not a comedy,
though the experience of Edward Blancove is
liable to the application of a comic moral of the
kind with which the fabulist ever concludes his
edifying tale. The central interest of the book
lies in the tragic seriousness of Dahlia's fate.
There is no book of Meredith's in which the mere

outcome is more constantly the chief concern of
the reader.   And there is no book of Meredith's
in which he makes more liberal use of the current
devices of melodrama.   That is, no doubt, one
reason for Stevenson's peculiar devotion to it.
I need only mention the exciting coincidences of
the final chapters.   Meredith is well aware of the
nature of these incidents, as the title-heads show:
"When the night is darkest—Dawn is near."
"Rhoda Fleming" is a masterpiece, but not a
masterpiece in Meredith's peculiar vein of comic
analysis of character.

There is, however, much humor and shrewdly
observed human nature in the secondary characters.   Mrs. Sumfit, Master Gammon and Mrs.
Boulby are all of the type of simple, good-hearted
people that go by the name of Dickens characters.
But these persons in " Rhoda Fleming " are never
caricatures, never do they o'erstep the modesty
of nature.   These funny rustics are unobtrusive
and thoroughly assimilated to the whole.   They
represent in the picture the tea and dumplings of
life.   And there lacks not the pathos that goes
with this paternally indulgent humor.   If the
generosity of the poor can touch the human heart,
it must do so in the gift to Dahlia of their
long-accumulated hoards by Mrs. Sumfit and

Master Gammon. There is more noble and moving pathos here than in the death of a child.

But this is not specially distinctive of Meredith. Many readers will prefer the rustic humors of Hardy; and we are all familiar in George Eliot with a tender pathos playing over obscure lives. A more imaginative and unusual creation is Anthony Hackbut. He is at once a type and an individual. He is not a mere humor in the Jonsonian sense, but is a rationalized and motived character, at least worthy of Balzac. A parsimonious bank-clerk, this simple little man is not in reality a miser. But he is willing to be thought so; and his whole ideal life comes to consist in his falsely estimated financial importance in the eyes of his brother-in-law. The tragedy of his life is the discovery by Fleming of his real insignificance. To us it is half comic, half pathetic, his appearance at the farm after the puncturing of his air-bubble. Formerly swollen with the dignity of his imputed riches, he is now a poor, shrunken, slinking creature, chiefly concerned to escape the observation of the farmer. The life is in fact gone out of him, and this is a mere ghost of himself. Grotesquely funny is the scene of his attempted escape from the farmhouse, hastily dressed in

whatever he could find. "Wrinkled with incongruous clothing from head to foot, and dazed
with the light, he peered on them, like a mouse
magnified and petrified."

Most picturesque is the scene of his meeting
with Rhoda, when the money demon has carried
him off with the bags of gold entrusted to his care.
Poor faithful servant of the bank, at last betrayed
by his imagination! He is greatly embarrassed
by Rhoda's demand for money. It is not so
much his crime that haunts him; but he dare not
confess to Fleming's daughter that he is not the
golden man she thinks. He delights in her wonder at the weight of the bags. And finally he
"slit the sides of the bags, and held them aloft,
and let the gold pour out in torrents, insufferable
to the sight; and uttering laughter that clamoured
fierily in her ears for long minutes afterwards, the
old man brandished the empty bags, and sprang
out of the room. She sat dismayed in the centre
of a heap of gold."

The spirit of comedy has been here to rarefy
the melodrama. This is a strange scene, on the
outer borders of the possible, it may be; but the
psychology is convincing. The play of motives
is clearly and poetically conceived. And the
whole career of Anthony Hackbut is a priceless

example of fantastic comedy leagues remote from the commonplace.

The "Tale of Chloe" is a work in which comedy and poetry are curiously blended. Although ending in suicide, this tale begins in a vein of burlesque, and a spirit of comedy prevails almost to the end. There is intense dramatic situation, pervasive dramatic irony, and there is at least one character conceived with the strangeness and beauty of poetic imagination. Chloe, the mysterious friend of Beau Beamish, tyrant of the Wells, has sojourned there for seven years, awaiting the promised return of her lover. To faithfulness in love she adds a charm of manner in society hardly surpassed among Meredith's heroines. For "she became the comrade of men without forfeit of her station among sage sweet ladies." It is to her care that Beau Beamish entrusts the Duchess Susan, when the aged Duke sends her to the Wells for a month's outing, on the Beau's pledge that she shall not come to harm. She is a young and ingenuous milkmaid exalted to noble rank, and of a natural liveliness giving promise of mischief. Coincident with her arrival is that of the long-awaited lover of Chloe; and the reader soon learns that here lies the menace of tragedy. While pretending faithful-

ness to Chloe, he is really making love to the
Duchess Susan.

It is not our business here to set forth the
tragedy of Chloe,—how she deliberately wraps
herself in illusion for the sake of a month's melancholy happiness; how free she shows herself from
jealousy and envy; and how in the end she offers
her life a sacrifice to save her charge from disgrace
and crime.   It is sufficient to point out the rare
blend of comic and tragic,—the dramatic irony
of the final scenes.   The workings of selfishness
in the bosom of the pastoral duchess are set forth
by the author with the pitiful tenderness of
Chloe's own feeling.   On the night when she is
going to betray her friend, the little duchess tries
not to think of her own unfaithfulness.

"She rushed on Chloe, kissed her hastily, de-
claring that she was quite dead of fatigue, and
dismissed her.   .   .   .
    " 'Another kiss,' Chloe said tenderly.
    " 'Yes, take it'—the duchess leaned her cheek
—'but I'm so tired I don't know what I'm doing.'
    " 'It will not be on your conscience,' Chloe
answered, kissing her warmly.
    "With these words she withdrew, and the
duchess closed the door.   She ran a bolt in it
immediately.
    " 'I'm too tired to know anything I'm doing,'
she said to herself, and stood with shut eyes to
hug certain thoughts that set her bosom heaving."

When Chloe said, "It will not be on your conscience," she knew the intentions of the duchess,
and the reader marvels at the forgiving and
charitable spirit of the lady, while he feels a pitiful scorn for human nature as exhibited in the
betrayer. A moment later he learns the full
import of Chloe's words, and he realizes the ironic
double meaning. The *act* of betrayal will never
be on the conscience of Susan. That is prevented
by her encounter with the dead body of Chloe.

Meantime the comic spirit follows with in-
exorable inquisition the mental struggles of that
naïve nature through the night of waiting. In
the midst of the distress of moral indecision, she
was yet clear-headed enough to safeguard ap-
pearances. "Providently she thumped a pillow,
and threw the bedclothes into proper disorder,
to inform the world that her limbs had warmed
them, and that all had been impulse with her."

In the "Tale of Chloe," we may distinguish
more than in any other of these "diversions" the
peculiar method of Meredith. A strange pathetic
story, conceived with rare beauty of poetic
imagination, not without suggestion of Jacobean
tragedy at its best, dramatic and striking in
effect: nevertheless, the prevailing interest of the
story lies perhaps in the analysis of motives,

in the comic delineation of character. Chloe
herself seems exempt from this inquisition; but
upon all the others the "spirit overhead" looks
"humanely malign," and casts "an oblique light
on them, followed by volleys of silvery laughter."
No story better illustrates the kinship of poetry
and comedy as children of the same creative
imagination. If it is the least read of Meredith's
stories, it is because this combination is so novel
in fiction. It constitutes a rareness exactly opposed to the commonplaceness by which "Diana"
has made itself the best read of all Meredith's
works.

CHAPTER XI

BRUNETIÈRE has a remarkable essay on the Philosophy of Molière.[1] The plays of Molière, he informs us, are to be understood as the expression of a distinct philosophy of life. He is the apostle of "Nature." His main comic types are chosen for laughing-stocks because they have set themselves contrary to nature.

One who attempts to form a systematic theory of the ludicrous finds himself much interested in this view of Molière; and is merely inclined to interpose a remark, that the unnatural,—that is, the absurd, the incongruous,—may be considered root of the ludicrous in general. Hence, one would say, any character contrary to nature is in so far comic, and *chooses himself* for comic treatment. The great value of the comic writer lies in the fact that he is the apostle of nature.

But the French critic uses the word nature in a peculiar sense, and the apostle of nature turns

[1] "Études critiques sur l'histoire de la littérature française."

183

out to be for him the most vicious of persons.
Molière, in an age of great Christian writers, is
himself no Christian. He continues the renaissance traditions of "nature." He is a forerunner
of Voltaire and Rousseau. These names are
uttered by the pious critic in the hushed voice
with which Wordsworth speaks of finding a
volume of Voltaire in the haunt of his Solitary.
These are the forerunners of our present day
materialists, all apostles of nature. The critic
recalls the bohemian life of this actor and stage
manager, enumerates the loose connections of his
life on the road and in Paris, and traces all this
license to the un-Christian education of his youth.
The plays are an appeal for license. "Tartuffe,"
the critic maintains, is not an exposure of hypoc-
risy but an attack upon piety,—that is, upon
clean living; and it was supported by the licentious young king because it condoned his own
vicious practice. This is that nature of which
Molière was the apostle.

Was ever the name of our common mother so
profaned? Nature, in the use of Brunetière, is
simply license. He does not inform us of this
identity of meanings. No more does he let us
know that clean living and religious faith are
identical. These equations he takes for granted,

because, as he would say, he is a Christian. Because, as we perceive, he is ready to repudiate
the faith of his own generation.[1]

However, I suspect a conformity, in these assumptions of Brunetière, with the usage of his
nation, or at least of many of his literary con-
frères. It is like the way in which French critics
are prone to confound a scientific view of human
development with determinism, pessimism, black
despair and *mal du siècle*.[2] Science, *we* say,
will inform us how to improve the breed. That
way lies hope. The *mal du siècle*, as we conceive, comes simply of ignoring the laws of nature.
Thus Meredith writes of Byron's Manfred as a
comic figure:

> "The cities, not the mountains, blow
>   Such bladders; in their shapes confessed
>   An after-dinner's indigest." [3]

[1] "Let us remember," says the "Pilgrim's Scrip," "that
Nature, the heathen, reaches at her best to the footstool
of the Highest. She is not all dust, but a living portion of
the spheres. In aspiration it is our error to despise her,
forgetting that only through Nature can we *ascend*.
Cherished, trained, and purified, she is then partly worthy
the divine mate who is to make her wholly so. St. Simeon
saw the Hog in Nature, and took Nature for the Hog."

[2] Of this age, as Meredith writes,
    "Its learning is through Science to despair."
And he goes on,
    "Despair lies down to grovel, grapples not
      With evil," etc.
("Foresight and Patience.")

[3] "Manfred." For other expression of anti-Byronism see

One of the French critics, most scientific of them all, writes prophetically of the literature of the future. He has done with Byron and his bad attack of the secular malady. He proceeds to set forth the diverse remedies now offered for man's disharmony by artist, Christian and worldly man. "There is another more profound," he goes on to say, "which Goethe was the first to propose, which we now begin to divine, towards which tend all the labor and all the experience of the century, and which may be the theme of the litera-ture to come: 'Try to understand thyself, and to understand nature.' " [1]

Try to understand thyself, and to understand nature. That is the theme of Meredith in all his writings, prose and verse.

And that nature does not mean license he tells us on every page. He of the Empty Purse was brought up suddenly in his licentious course against the hard handling of nature; and then first the poet conceived hope for him. Nature

"Beauchamp," IV; and observe that Byron was the favorite poet of Mrs. Marsett!

[1] "Il y a une autre plus profonde que Goethe a faite le premier, que nous commençons à soupçonner, où aboutis-sent tout le travail et toute l'expérience du siècle, et qui sera peut-être la matière de la littérature prochaine: 'Tâche de te comprendre et de comprendre les choses.' " Taine, "Histoire de la Littérature anglaise," Book IV, chap. II, vi.

would discipline him.   License does indeed mask
under the name of nature—

"Delicious licence called it Nature's cry.

But the true goddess Nature demands the observance of her laws:

"Obedient to Nature, not her slave:
  Her lord, if to her rigid laws he bows;
  Her dust, if with his conscience he plays knave,
  And bids the Passions on the Pleasures browse."

These lines occur in the remarkable poem, the
"Test of Manhood," the last of a series of poems
in which Meredith tries to adjust the rival claims
of puritan and voluptuary, and in which matters
of the greatest delicacy are handled freely with
an ingenious good taste unparalleled perhaps in
verse.   Artemis and Aphrodite, the Huntress and
the Persuader, stand respectively for work and
pleasure, self-restraint and indulgence, chastity
and love.   The introductory poem assures us
that both elements must be present in healthy
character.   Neither goddess must we shun;
neither must we too devoutly follow.   The two
succeeding poems celebrate, one the exhilarating
joys offered by Artemis, the other the voluptuous
and wholesome pleasures of Aphrodite.   The
"Test of Manhood" then describes the development of character from the strife of these two

powers in man's breast. Man's task is to
reconcile the foes, or strike a balance between
them. Both he must serve.

> "Back to the primal brute shall he retrace
> His path, doth he permit to force her chains
> A soft Persuader coursing through his veins,
> An icy Huntress stringing to the chase."

This is but a modern way of recommending the
favorite ancient virtue of temperance. This discipline has been the means of civilizing man,
according to the poet, and is to be the instrument
of his further refinement.

In the matter of sex relations, Meredith realizes
that the line of morality is not absolutely identical
with that of legal and religious sanction. But
this does not mean that he condones license. In
two of his later novels, he has introduced marriage
relations extra-legal. In these books he does not
attempt to solve all the problems involved. One
may be sure there is nothing sacred to him in the
mere religious or legal countenance of conjugal
union. The obligation is a moral one. As to
its binding force, each case must be decided on its
own merits. There is no condemnation of his
Aminta for her violation of the marriage vow.
In that case, the husband had long since forfeited
his claims by repudiation of the wife's.

But the case of Victor Radnor is not so simple.
The whole narrative might seem intended as a
demonstration of the impracticability of such
illegal unions, in view of the social handicap im-
posed upon the offspring. The catastrophe would
seem to imply a condemnation of Victor's life
with Nataly. We are told that, in the end, "for
the cancelling of the errors chargeable to them,
the father and mother had kept good faith with
Nature." Of these errors, however, the illegal
marriage was not the greatest; there was nothing
unnatural in that. The first great violation of
nature was Victor's marrying old Mrs. Burman
for her money. The next great error was, as we
have seen, in his refusal to accept the conditions
created by his illegal union. And there followed
his dishonest attempt to impose his daughter
upon a man who did not realize her social dis-
ability.

Victor was led to this obviously immoral procedure by his lack of trust in nature. He and
Nataly had invoked nature for their own benefit without any strong faith in her. They had
appealed to nature as a power superior to social
convention. They had preferred the deep and
real gratifications of affectionate wedlock to the
sanction of the world. And yet they craved, like

any worldlings, the stamp of popular approval. Nataly was so thoroughly subject to the conventional standards that she could doubt the purity of her own daughter on hearing that she had shown compassionate interest in an unfortunate woman. She imagined her daughter as without reputation, conceiving how the world would associate the character of the daughter with the unhallowed life of the mother. "She had in her wounded breast the world's idea, that corruption must come of the contact with impurity." "The mother—the daughter!" she cried to herself, invaded and subdued by the world. Though Victor was not tortured in this fashion, he did continue to struggle for the tinsel prize of the world's regard.

That Meredith does not propose nature as a substitute for moral obligation is obvious throughout the book. In the companionship of Lady Grace, Victor was inclined to think of nature as a devouring element, "uproarious in her primitive licentiousness." But he learned that mere natural instinct is not to be taken for the great goddess herself. "He began, under the influence of Nesta's companionship, to see the Goddess Nature there is in a chastened nature." [1]

[1] Compare what the author says of Nature in the loves

"One of Our Conquerors" cannot then be regarded as a brief for licentious nature that knows no law. Nature is the very incarnation of law; and a reasoned nature is the basis of morality. Victor and Nataly cannot be set forth as the true expositors of nature. On the contrary, Victor is a comic figure, as we have seen, just because of his perverse attempt to ignore the laws of nature; and his undertaking to walk on stilts beyond the contact of earth led to the deep and tragic fall. Victor Radnor, the Optimist, stands for the emotional view of things. He lacked mental discipline. But he received this sufficiently to grasp the difference between mere natural impulse and the reasoned nature which we call common sense, and which underlies morality.

This reasoned nature is the constant subject of Meredith in his poems. The discipline of character recommended in the "Test of Manhood" is a work of the mind, or reason,—itself a product of natural evolution, and to be cherished as such. Often as Meredith mentions Earth, or Nature, not less often does he mention, or have in view, Reason, Mind, Brain, Wisdom,—

of middle-aged people, who "show her to us discreet, civilized, in a decent moral aspect," etc., "General Ople and Lady Camper," VIII.

never as the adversary, but always the auxiliary,
or interpreter, of Nature.

> "Never is Earth misread by brain:
> That is the welling of her, there
> The mirror: with one step beyond,
> For likewise is it voice." [1]

The human brain is the mouthpiece of nature.
This does not mean that the brain, or mind,
merely records the desire of the senses. It is in
constant strife with these its parents. The poet's
chief aspiration is for the dominance of mind
over the senses.[2] Again and again he tells us
prophetically, in the "Reading of Earth," how

> "The rebel, the heart, yields place
> To brain, each prompting the soul—"

> "—from flesh unto spirit man grows
> Even here on the sod under sun." [3]

The flesh and the "rebel heart" are impatient of
the yoke of earth's law, but must be made to
submit to the discipline of mind.[4]

---

[1] "Hard Weather."
[2] "But that the senses still
    Usurp the station of their issue mind,
    He [man] would have burst the chrysalis of the blind:
    As yet he will." ("Earth and Man.")
[3] Both passages from "A Faith on Trial."
[4] "Reason, man's germinant fruit.
    She wrestles with our old worm
    Self in the narrow and wide:
    Relentless quencher of lies,
    With laughter she pierces the brute;

In this employment by Nature, mind, or reason, has many instruments; but foremost among them, in the view of Meredith, is the Comic Spirit, the Sword of Common Sense, whose business is the piercing of lies.   The prey of the Comic Spirit is ever the unnatural.   Every one of the follies enumerated in the "Essay on Comedy" constitutes in some sort a violation of nature.   Whenever, the critic says, men "wax out of proportion, overblown, affected, pretentious, bombastical, hypocritical, pedantic, fantastically delicate; whenever it [the Comic Spirit] sees them self-deceived or hoodwinked, given to run riot in idolatries, drifting into vanities, congregating in absurdities, planning shortsightedly, plotting dementedly; whenever they are at variance with their professions, and violate the unwritten but perceptible laws binding them in consideration one to another; whenever they offend sound reason, fair justice; are false in humility or mined with conceit, individually, or in the bulk—the Spirit overhead will look humanely malign and cast an oblique light on them, followed by volleys of silvery laughter.   That is the Comic Spirit."

And hear we her laughter peal,
'Tis light in us dancing to scour
The loathed recess of his dens."   ("A Faith on Trial.")

Of all these forms of contrariness to nature, Meredith gives plentiful illustration in his novels. Some violation of nature is practised by each one of his great comic figures. Nature is, to be sure, a somewhat protean word as used by Meredith; but the various meanings point always in the same direction. By virtue of his mental faculty of invention, man is prone to build up artificial systems not based on the universal laws of being. With the word nature Meredith keeps referring him back to these laws that govern the movements of our planet and the growth of organisms. The human heart, teeming with whimsical aspirations, takes no account of what is possible and consistent; and the reason must be called upon to read the heart a lesson in law. Meredith is an unmistakable contemporary of Darwin. He wishes man never to forget his blood-relationship to the other orders of living things. And while he will not have him take excuse from his origin for a display of brutal passions, he bids him have in mind the necessary conditions inherent in his animal nature. Common sense may be described as the faculty of interpreting these conditions. In "Sandra Belloni," the Philosopher has been describing the character of Hippogriff, the steed of sentiment. "Let him repeat at the same time," says the author, "that souls harmonious to Nature, of whom there are few, do not mount this animal. . . . You will mark in them a reverence for the laws of their being, and a natural obedience to common sense." [1]

Sir Austin is a general representative of men who become ridiculous in the effort to thwart nature. His system is a counterpart of the systems of Arnolphe and Sganarelle, and is still more unreasonable as applied to a young man. Sir Austin would erect a science that takes no account of instinct, that is actually opposed to instinct as a rival; and we have the gratification of watching the triumph of instinct at the very moment when fatuous Science is most complacent over its own proceedings. For all that was done in the name of Science was done in violation of Nature.

The snob is unnatural in a somewhat different sense. He follows an instinct natural enough in wishing to enjoy the regard of his fellows. But the snob is unnatural, and comic, in his cultivation

[1] Compare also what the author says in "Celt and Saxon," VI, about "situations of grisly humour, where certain of the passions of man's developed nature are seen armed and furious against our mild prevailing mother nature; and the contrast between our utter wrath and her simple exposition of the circumstances and consequences forming her laws."

of specious values,—dignities not recognized in
the aristocracy of nature, shall we say? or dignities abhorrent to the true democracy of nature.
Louisa Harrington is a more ridiculous M. Jour-
dain: more ridiculous because she would per-
petuate an artificial distinction that was in her
day obsolete, or obsolescent, as she might have
learned from the experience of her own family.

But the snob is not the species discovered and
first described by Meredith; and the Book of
Snobs has less significance for his philosophy than
any other part of his work.   In his more serious
novels, the commonest theme is sentimentality;
and it is in the delineation of this vice that he
makes most frequent appeal to "nature."   The
sentimental snob is more unnatural than the plain
variety, flying one circle higher, one remove farther from common sense.   The perversity of the
Pole sisters is seen most strikingly in their contempt for money.   For in despising this, the fine
ladies cut themselves off from the breast of nature.[1]

[1] Even more obviously than these sentimentalists a
rebel against nature is Astræa, the "dedicated widow" in
the play.   Though she feels the natural motions of love
towards young Arden, she is ashamed to acknowledge
them; for she thinks herself bound to maintain her ideal of
devotion to a husband whom she had possessed for two
months and mourned for two years.   It is a theme congenial to the author of "A Reading of Earth" and "A
Reading of Life."

The sentimentalist in love is especially dangerous, inasmuch as he handles such dangerous
weapons. He regards love as a pretty toy, not
as a powerful engine for good or bad. He would
pervert nature by producing a flower without
fruit. He would enjoy the agreeable stimuli from
his senses, but inhibit the muscular response.
Science tells us that nature will have her revenge
upon one who makes this separation between feeling and act. It will be made a permanent divorce.

The sentimentalist is so alien to nature that he
does not recognize true natural beauty, but is
always craving some artificial refinement, some
impossible romance. This was the blindness of
Wilfrid Pole and the Earl of Fleetwood. These
would not acknowledge nature; and they put
her off so long that in the end she would not
acknowledge them. When they appealed to Love
for admission to his enchanted garden, Love replied, "I know you not." Fleetwood in particular, under the influence of his religious friend,
had a distrust of nature in the person of Venus.
He was a subscriber to the doctrine of Sir Austin,
fearing woman as the origin of evil and the great
disturber of tranquillity. And to measure his
folly the author makes more than usually frequent
reference to the standards of nature.

Sir Willoughby made dishonest use of the
natural passion of love to cover another order of
passions. He is the most broadly typical of
Meredith's figures, and illustrates the essential
divorce from nature of the civilized egoist. The
thorough egoist is incapable of the passion of love
in its full sense. For the grand passion requires
a forgetfulness of self, a surrender of the limited
interests of the individual to the larger purposes
of nature. The grand passion does not select its
object with deliberate calculation of the worldly
advantage involved. It follows an instinct more
sure than that. Sir Willoughby wished a wife
who would be worthy of the station she must
assume as his lady. In choosing Clara Middleton
he could see the telescopes of all gentlemen turned
enviously upon his moon. This is not the way
of the grand passion. Its votaries are victims
transfixed by the dart of beauty. Or, to adopt
another figure from its poetical exponents, they
are drawn like the turbulent ocean with irre-
sistible power towards the orb that controls them.
The language of the passion has become familiar.
"One word is too often profaned." Everyone
that can read has command of the vocabulary of
love. Sir Willoughby is more than commonly
eloquent. No humility restrains him; no vio-

lence of feeling chokes his voice. He makes love with the easy fervency of the tenor in Italian opera. He never, as a matter of fact, shows signs of being in love with anyone but himself.

While it is in connection with romantic sentiment that the comic is seen most unmistakably to be one with the unnatural, I think the same relation may be traced in connection with the civilized egoist in general. If the equation here seem fanciful and far-sought, it is at least in harmony with the spirit of Meredith, and serves to make more conspicuous the singleness of his philosophy. The egoist must be recommended, like every other perverse character, to the mild and sensible admonitions of Mother Nature.

The egoist may seem to be the very type of the natural. Egoism is the force by which the individual asserts himself and fulfils his natural instincts. But the instincts of the "social egoist" are not all natural; they are not all properly instincts. They partake of the artificiality of snobbish and sentimental aspirations. And there is something suicidal in the way in which the social egoist cuts himself off from the most intimate joys of social life. Nature, we might say, has regard for the type, the race; she prefers society to the individual. But the duties of the

individual she makes privileges. The highest
pleasure possible to a human being is to function
well as a member of society. The egoist declines
to be a part of the social organism. He will have
his own way regardless of those about him. And
like the snob, he mistakes husk for kernel. He
chooses the specious gratifications of wilful vanity
before the deep and real gratifications of service
and affection. He gives up the better part of
his own nature. And so of his pattern of egoistic
humanity, Meredith writes, rising into verse for
the better pointing of the wit,

"Through very love of self himself he slew."

"Let it be admitted for his epitaph," says the
author of Sir Willoughby. Let it be admitted for
the epitaph of each of these followers of will o' the
wisp, whether in the category of snob, sentimentalist or egoist.

In this study we consider only the comic side of
Meredith's genius. We are therefore concerned
only with those characters in whom is set forth
the folly of antagonism to nature. This is the
negative side of the shield. The doctrine of
nature may be as strikingly inculcated through
characters harmonious with nature. And a great
distinction of Meredith consists in his maintain-

ing the balance of comic and exemplary figures. The contrast of Lady Camper and General Ople, with the comic discipline of the latter by the former, has its counterpart in nearly every one of his novels. Above all, Emilia and Carinthia stand for the fair and noble simplicity of nature.

Vernon Whitford and Gower Woodseer are in contrast to Sir Willoughby and Fleetwood by virtue of their sturdy and conscious cultivation of nature. Especially interesting is the temptation of Woodseer in relation to the Countess Livia, when his "imagination, foreign to his desires and his projects, was playing juggler's tricks with him." Woodseer is made to marry the servant Madge as a practical instance of a natural union. She had shown herself an ideal woman, possessed of courage, honesty, devotedness, enthusiasm. But she had none of the glamour of rank and queenliness that hung about the weak-willed Countess. She was plain, sweet, wholesome nature, a dish unspiced. Woodseer is constantly preaching his natural philosophy to the deluded romantic earl. "Love Nature, she makes you lord of her boundless, off any ten square feet of earth. I go through my illusions and come always back on that good truth. It says, beware of the world's passion for flavours

and spices." Fleetwood was offended by woman's
animal nature.

" 'Such animals these women are! Good Lord!'
Fleetwood ejaculated. 'I marry one, and I'm to
take to reading medical books!' He yawned.
" 'You speak that of women and pretend to
love Nature,' said Gower. 'You hate Nature
unless you have it served on a dish by your own
cook. . . . A man finds the woman of all
women fitted to stick him in the soil, and trim
and point him to grow, and she's an animal for
her pains! The secret of your malady is, you've
not yet . . . hopped to the primary conception of what Nature means. Women are in and
of Nature.' "

The teaching of Gower Woodseer in the last of
Meredith's comic studies is in agreement with
that of Mrs. Berry in the first. And the teaching
of all these novels is not different from that of
the poems. Mr. Le Gallienne has made the
brilliant guess that George Meredith is an incarnation of the God Pan. There cannot be a
doubt of this. Nature is everywhere the key-
word of his gospel. To learn to live by nature is,
he believes, the present lesson set for human
kind. Comedy has its place here as indicating
the absurdity of the unnatural.

The main business of comedy is destruction.
It is engaged for the exposure of humbug and
nonsense. But in that capacity, it is a mere

auxiliary in the fight for better things. No one insists on this more emphatically than Meredith, who worships the comic spirit as the bringer of light and restorer of harmony. It is seldom Meredith leaves us in the woods with no hint of a way out. He is no riddling Ibsen. Even his abortive Beauchamp is a noble fragment of political hero. His true women are always full compensation for his vain men. Matey Weyburn and Aminta, Clara Middleton and Vernon Whitford, lift torches upon the dark road of humanity.

Considered in the larger sense, comedy is the agent of civilization. "She is the ultimate civilizer, the polisher, a sweet cook." [1] The comic spirit is a republican, leading the race to a true brotherhood through harmony with nature. By the analysis of discord she teaches the laws of harmony. She is therefore "verily Keeper of the Muse's key,"

"Holding, as she, all dissonance abhorred;

And teaching how for being subjected free
Past thought of freedom we may come to know
The music of the meaning of Accord." [2]

The comic philosophy of Meredith is thus not to be distinguished from the teaching of his work

[1] Prelude to the "Egoist."
[2] "Ode to the Comic Spirit."

as a whole.   Conformity to nature is the key to
action, and its object is the good of the race.
Meredith has always his eyes on the future.
They rest on the snow-capped and rose-hued
mountains forward.   The song of Vittoria soars
to nobler heights than mere national patriotism.

> "For all Humanity doth owe a debt
> To all Humanity, until the end."

It is interesting to observe that "Vittoria," as
well as five other novels of Meredith, and numer-
ous poems and essays, appeared first in the
"Fortnightly Review," which might almost have
been called the organ of the positivists: men
doubtless abhorrent to the spirit of Brunetière;
men earnest in the effort to construct a philosophy
of nature, and devoted to the cause of humanity.
The faith and passion of humanity runs all
through Meredith's poems, and is the undertone
of his novels.   Let none call this man cynic.
Read what scornful things he has to say of that
character.   He would not choose, I think, to be
labelled optimist; but he has nothing in common
with the pessimist.   He has the calm serenity of
nature, bred of the knowledge of good and evil,
of long and far views.   Let none call him un-
believer that has not a saner and robuster faith

than he. Does he not declare the noblest philosophy of our day?—a philosophy neither cynic nor stoic, though so bravely self-denying.

And the sum of his teaching is an inspiration. For he has faith in his method, and looks to the future with courage and confidence.

"By my faith, there is feasting to come,
  Not the less, when our earth we have seen
  Beneath and on surface, her deeds and designs:
  Who gives us the man-loving Nazarene,
  The martyrs, the poets, the corn and the vines.
  By my faith in the head, she has wonders in
      loom;
  Revelations, delights. I can hear a faint crow
  Of the cock of fresh mornings, far, far, yet
      distinct." [1]

[1] "The Empty Purse."

CHAPTER XII

THERE is an evolution and progress in Meredith's employment of the comic method. Starting out with a liberal use of the waggish and fantastic, he displays something of the exuberance and effervescence of the professional humorist.[1] Gradually his fancy is disciplined to a more exclusive pursuit of the essential comic theme, and he produces significant pictures of life, well designed and closely considered. Generally, however, in his earlier stories, he confines himself to fairly obvious comic traits, not attempting a very close analysis of the subtleties of character. So that these stories are rather light and amusing,

[1] The four tales of the "Story-telling Party" (printed in "Once A Week," for Christmas, 1859) are not recognizable, either in substance or style, as by the author of "Richard Feverel." The "Dreadful Night in a Hut on the Moors" presents one of those scenes of fisticuffs and confusion so frequent in "Peregrine Pickle" and "Joseph Andrews." The two following stories are in the picaresque vein. Perhaps one may discover in the "Terrible Day in a Railway Carriage" a faint suggestion of the author of the chapter in "One of Our Conquerors" on the lapdog Tasso.

and the laughter not more thoughtful than consists with recreative entertainment. But he soon
develops a more than usually serious conception
of comedy, and a comic method that involves a
searching study of motives, laying bare unsus-
pected and curious veins of self-deceit and affectation. He cannot at once master so difficult and
novel a comic method. "Sandra Belloni" gives
record of experimentation. The "Essay on
Comedy" shows him busy in the development of
his ideal. In the "Egoist," he has for the first
time successfully applied his novel instrument to
the production of an effective and beautiful work
of art. The comedies that follow are not so well
conceived. He did not always succeed in finding
a clear and effective medium for the conveyance
of his idea. In his final work of fiction he did
succeed; and the "Amazing Marriage" has a
distinction of its own that gives it high rank
among works of art.

Meredith's undertaking is bold, original, and
well-nigh superhuman. He was a pioneer, map-
ping out new country. Artistically he was not
always quite sure of his whereabouts. Not all
his stories are effective as art. Of the comedies
that stand out as notably successful there are
three: "Evan Harrington," the "Egoist," and

the "Amazing Marriage." In these books there
is an approach to completeness in the execution
of difficult designs; and the reader of taste delights in perfection of form, revels in the sense of
masterful accomplishment. The other comedies
are less happily designed or less gratifying in
execution; and while we may be deeply interested
in the subject-matter, and pleased with details of
artistic virtuosity or imaginative splendor, there
is not the same fulness of satisfaction in the
general effect.

I do not include in this comparison those delicious *hors d'œuvre*, the stories of Mart Tinman
and General Ople. The latter is the most laughable of Meredith's stories, and contains scenes
of misunderstanding worthy of Molière. The
"House on the Beach" is more a product of the
imagination. I have a great fondness for this
curious tale, which seems, like the "Tale of
Chloe," to be laid in a strange unfamiliar world
of dreams and consistent unrealities. There is no
stress upon the comic traits, and the general effect
is that of water color as compared with oil paint-
ing. Though the character of Mart Tinman is
one proper to the pen of Dickens, he is not treated
as Dickens would have treated him. Always the
author stops short of the call for explosive laugh-

ter, restraining himself within the limits of verisimilitude. What he loses in breadth and
vividness of effect, he gains in plausibility and
consistency. This tale was contemporary with
the "Essay on Comedy," and manifests a refinement and sureness of touch not commanded by
the author at the start. The style and conception
of "Farina" are both most crude in comparison.
Much of it is written with an impertinent smart-
ness suggestive of Mr. Bernard Shaw. The
conclusion is in the style of Gilbert and Sullivan.
"Farina" is a good story of adventure spoiled
by frivolous treatment. There is fun in it. But
it falls below the notice of the Comic Muse.

"Richard Feverel" is not in the comparison
because it is hardly a comedy. There will be few
to regret this accident; for have we not, one says,
something nobler than comedy?

Something similar is true of "Harry Richmond," the most romantic of Meredith's novels.
One might suppose it an adventure story until
more than half through; the events move with
the kaleidoscopic swiftness and variety of a tale
of Borrow or Smollett. It proves to be more a
Bildungsroman than a story of adventure; but
the hero is rather a faint personality, and the
centre of interest is the bizarre and picturesque

figure of Richmond Roy: a poetic creation in the
manner of Shakespeare and Cervantes. Richmond Roy is not conceived in the dry light of
comedy, like Alceste, Mr. Darcy, Sir Willoughby.
We see him first through the eyes of a child,
grandiose by reason of that magnifying medium.
The absurdity of his manner in the opening scene
is given a touch of unreality by the romantic
chiaroscuro of that midnight setting. We are
next introduced to the charms of Richie's father
as an entertainer. Naturally, one whose views of
himself and society were as childlike as those of
Richmond Roy could strike the note most sympathetic to a child's fancy. And his personal
charm was a real one. He had the mercurial
spirits of a child. He was really a poet, or
chameleon to all the sentiments that make
life colorful. "No one talked, looked, flashed,
frowned, beamed as he did! No one was ever
so versatile in playfulness. He took the colour
of the spirits of the people about him." Richmond Roy is celebrated with the pen of a poet.
"Gaiety," sings the poet, "sprang under his
feet."

The portrait of Richmond Roy is a splendid
creation of pictorial fancy. But of all the early
comedies, the most successful dramatically is

"Evan Harrington." There is, I presume, less difference of opinion in regard to "Evan Harrington" than in regard to any other novel of Meredith. No one considers it supremely great, and no one questions its effectiveness. It presents no difficulties to the least earnest or least clever of readers. A touch of the snob makes the whole world kin. The plot is at the same time most ingenious and yet simple and direct. The story really divides itself into scenes for the stage. But in spite of the originality of the plot, the general effect might border on Victorian commonplaceness were it not for the invention of the great Mel. This quaint ghostly personage, stalking the footsteps of his ungrateful children, lends a touch of poetry to the whole. By the help of the great Mel, the story vindicates itself as a work of imagination.

This was not, however, what Meredith most wanted to achieve. In my opinion, the great triumphs of his comic genius are among the more serious novels of the later period, following the "Essay on Comedy."

Already in his third novel he was reaching out in that direction; and "Sandra Belloni" will tell us more of what Meredith was after than any novel before the "Egoist." But the book must

be acknowledged a failure as a work of art.
Besides the inconclusiveness of the story, it is a
failure because Meredith attempted in it more
than could be compassed in a single novel.   There
is no book in which you will find more frequent
and more diverting passages of humor.   It is the
very wealth that embarrasses the reader.   The
plot is too complex, and involves too many important characters.   The reader's interest is
divided, and his understanding confused.   But
there is another fault that strikes deeper.   The
author has undertaken to analyze and set forth
certain varieties of sentimental self-deception
more subtle than any comic traits with which he
has yet dealt.   And he has not entirely succeeded
in giving dramatic embodiment to his comic
abstractions.   On occasions, the analysis of character is almost wholly divorced from action.
The philosopher takes the stage to lecture on the
nature of Hippogriff, and we are left to wonder
at the *à-propos*.   The puppets are not animated
with the breath of life.

Not till the "Egoist" did Meredith employ this
close analytic method with artistic success.   The
"Egoist" is perfectly simple in plan: a single
unified action, and a single comic protagonist,
who takes the centre of the stage and holds it from

the rise to the fall of the curtain. The reader is at once advised what should be his attitude towards Sir Willoughby, and is never left in doubt as to the issues. The drama moves forward with steady sureness and without interruption. The movement accelerates, and the interest deepens, to the end. The conclusion is neat and final. And yet, the simplicity of plot consists with a great amount of action, with complexity of motives, and a wealth of comic misunderstanding and suspense. There is sufficient material for three comedies that could not be branded "talky." In every dialogue, there is a clearly defined and momentous issue. I can think of no scene in drama more exciting than that in the Patterne library, in which Clara begs her father first to go and then to stay. Sir Willoughby displays in this scene all the devilish ingenuity of the stage villain; and the courage and strength of the heroine are taxed to the utmost to make head against his urgency. This one scene would make the reputation of a clever actress.

But the action is not devised merely for its own sake. Generally a comic situation is brought about with little reference to the involutions of human psychology. Sganarelle and Arnolphe, Falstaff and Malvolio, are made to accomplish

their own humiliation by mere tricks on the part
of their opponents, and mere density on their
own part. Or a study of human nature for its
own sake is made with a practical abandonment
of dramatic action or dénouement, as in the
"Misanthrope." In the "Egoist," we have both
dramatic action and psychological analysis,—
each in fullest development, and in completest
harmony. The author, while he takes delight in
the public embarrassment of his victim, in the
practical application of comic justice, is mainly
concerned with the motives and moral processes
by which the action comes about; and he has
never forced the psychology for the sake of the
action. For once, in a comedy, the plot is actually the flowering out of character. And the
analysis of motives is here a natural accompani-
ment of the action, which stands upon its own
feet. The chief exposition of Sir Willoughby's
character is made in the record of his relations
to Clara Middleton. He is seen through the eyes
of his bride, who studies him, and forms her
opinion of him through his words and acts. In
their dialogue, the author gives full dramatic
embodiment to the minutely distinguished refinements of egoism.

We have, therefore, in the "Egoist," a successful employment of methods that, in "Sandra Belloni," were not fully mastered by the artist. I do not feel that they were again employed with notable success till we come to the last of all the novels. The "Tragic Comedians" is not properly a work of fiction, and the author did not have sufficiently free play for his imagination. He felt bound to follow closely the actual lines of history. And while his interpretation is ingenious and unfailingly suggestive, we feel a want of body and verisimilitude. We are reminded of Aristotle's distinction between history, which records the facts as they did happen, and poetry, which sets forth what should have happened. Meredith has done his utmost to invest the incidents with poetical (that is, human) significance. I find myself illuminated, but not convinced. There is in the early chapters a brilliance of attack, a movement that sweeps one forward. Both characters are conceived with imaginative daring and shrewd grasp of human nature. But it cannot be denied that one-half the book is given up to psychological analysis pure and simple; and that the action is recorded after the manner of the historian rather than that of the novelist. We are *informed* of such and such an act, but we are not *shown* it. It is not bodied forth to our vision. The circumstances and setting are not given in sufficient detail to make us at home in the story.

What Meredith could not, or would not, do with a given series of historical events, he could accomplish by fictitious invention. And in "One of our Conquerors" he gives us another "Tragic Comedians" furnished with full complement of imaginative accessories. Too full indeed. Not only do we have Victor Radnor shown in his surroundings so completely that we could recognize him by his dress, his manner, his taste in music. Not only do we make the acquaintance of the others foremost in the drama. We never get to the end of of Skepsey's escapades or Colney Durance's satirical excursions; and we spend whole evenings and mornings with Pemptons and Priscillas. These episodic matters are treated with undue emphasis, so that the main lines of the action do not stand forth with that simplicity necessary to artistic effectiveness.

There is another feature of the novel which, though contributing to the humorous effect, adds another occasion for bewilderment. In no story does Meredith make more constant use of the comic method of indirection. By this I mean that way of narrating events and recording

mental processes from the point of view of the
dramatis personæ,—a dramatic self-projection of
the author into the minds of his characters. There
is a whimsical humor in this, as the reader of
Lamb and Richter and Carlyle knows well. But
there is much that is puzzling for the reader not
used to these nimble shiftings of the point of
view. He knows not where Carlyle leaves off
and Teufelsdröckh begins, or where Carlyle and
Teufelsdröckh are blended in one riot of half-
serious irony. This is a different matter from
the dramatic monologues of Browning, in which
the frank assumption of the first person advises
us of the transformation of the author into a
Caliban or an Italian person of quality. In
"One of our Conquerors," Meredith is much of
the time telling the story in the manner of Victor
Radnor or the other characters; but he still uses
the third person of the omniscient author, and
it is sometimes difficult to know how far he agrees
with the opinions of his creatures. Victor Radnor's estimate of his own character in the glow
of the Old Veuve is not the less the estimate of
Victor Radnor himself for being to a large extent
correct. It has the color of his own sanguine temperament, sympathetically taken by the author.
And yet there are no quotation marks. "Mr.

Radnor meanwhile scribbled, and despatched a strip of his Note-book, bearing a scrawl of orders, to his office. He was now fully himself, benevolent, combative, gay, alert for amusement or the probeing of schemes to the quick, weighing the good and the bad in them *with his fine touch on proportion.*" The italics are not Meredith's. He never underscores his pleasantries. Not even quotation marks; but in the final phrase, the irony peeps out. Especially in retrospect we have a vision of the light thrown upon this self-congratulation by the facts of his career; and we become aware of silvery laughter overhead.

This kind of playful masquerade is the very breath and fragrance of the essay, and of a certain order of humorous fiction. It has not permanently prevented the appreciation of Carlyle, being indeed appropriate to the sort of philosophical tentatives and adumbrations of truth in which he excels. In a dramatically designed and progressive story, it is not perhaps so appropriate. The psychology of Victor Radnor and his acquaintance is sufficiently involved, the elements of the story are sufficiently complex, without the addition of this humorous bewilderment of style. Whatever be the cause, "One of our Conquerors" gives the impression of over-

elaboration, undue richness of detail. It is "honey upon sugar, sugar upon honey." It is of the most serious interest as an essay in the remote confines of comedy. As a work of art, it cannot be pronounced a great success.

With the "Amazing Marriage," we arrive at a most effective as well as original performance. Once more we have the refined and serious comic method applied in a story of admirable simplicity and directness. The lively introductory chapters by Dame Gossip are not necessary to give the story a push, though we should not wish to miss their exhilarating drollery. The mountain walk in mist and sunshine launches the story proper with romantic picturesqueness and spirit. Curious interest and suspense are maintained straight on through the marriage of Fleetwood and Carin up to the time of the Whitechapel business. By this time we have come to know and love the heroine; and we are sufficiently piqued and curious about the man to go through considerable exposition of feelings without a murmur. A kidnapping, encounter with a mad dog, and the like, are incidents stirring enough to support the weight of analysis with which they are accompanied. The mere charm of Carinthia's personality, and the unusual interest of her story,

would float a heavier burden.   But there is never
any doubt as to the occasion for analysis.   The
refinements of epicurean sentiment express themselves naturally in act in the course of a plausible
and enthralling story;   and the action is inter-
preted to us with natural and appropriate comment.

Accordingly, the last of Meredith's novels takes
its place with "Evan Harrington" and the
"Egoist" as one of the three effective realistic
comedies.   It ranks higher than "Evan Harrington" in seriousness of theme, but is less
amusing.   It has a quality of rareness about it
not shared by the earlier novel, but will not make
so general an appeal as the more commonplace
production.   It does not strike so familiar a
chord in the experience of the average reader;
and it does not so readily suggest presentation
on the stage.

But the "Egoist" remains the masterpiece.
This central comedy combines the excellences
of the earlier and the later ones.   The subject is
as serious as that of any of Meredith's books,
though it does not share the grave seriousness
that shadows some of the later ones by reason of
the tragic issues.   The protagonist is a man of
social dignity and fair morality, though greatly

open to the shafts of the imps. He is as worthy a subject for comic treatment as the Misanthrope. In such a man, the comic traits of humanity are worth minute and careful study. Associated with him, and affected by his eccentric movements, are several other characters of weight, whose fortunes we follow with the deepest concern. But the "Egoist" has the advantage of leavening the seriousness of the later comedies with the amusing qualities of the early ones. The invincible conceit of Sir Willoughby, as we have seen, his desperate shifts and embarrassments, his self-delusion at the beginning of the story, and his vain ingenuities at the end, make him much more laughable than Fleetwood or Victor Radnor.

There are other points of excellence, charms and graces, peculiar to this book. An indefinable savor, product of many well-mingled ingredients, too well mingled for easy detection, is yet palpable to the sense of the epicure. The reader has never moved in more agreeable society. He has never lent his ear to more refined and graceful dialogue, proper to high comedy. A fair thread of ingenuous boyishness is run though the pattern by young Crossjay. There is a wistful droll pathos about Clara's flight in wild weather, and

her meek return to Patterne Hall. There is
something peculiarly gratifying in the way in
which at the end of the story Lætitia applies to
Sir Willoughby the epithet applied to him by
Clara at the beginning. They have both come
to think of him as an egoist. But Clara, in her
gratitude at being released, is generous and
humble; and it hurts her as much to hear him
called egoist now as once it hurt Lætitia. There
is something akin to wit in the recurrence of this
situation thus inverted,—a kind of long-distance
repartee. Or it might be more natural to compare it to the recurrence in the final movement
of a symphony of a motive declared at the beginning, but transposed into a different key. One
of the chief gratifications of the reader of Meredith comes with appreciation of the large organic
symmetries of design that underlie the seeming
capriciousness.

I have little doubt that the "Egoist" will become for English readers, what it is said to be
now for the French, the representative novel of
Meredith. If it be true that comedy was Meredith's characteristic genre, the "Egoist" must
be his masterpiece. It is at once the most perfect in design and the most comprehensive in
material of all his novels, and consequently of

all his works. We could lose everything else of
Meredith, and we should have in the "Egoist"
an epitome of his philosophy and his art. The
"Egoist" is to Meredith what "Hamlet" is to
Shakespeare.

INDEX

Arabic numerals refer to pages, roman numerals to chapters.
In the case of the latter, the topic will be found treated *passim*
in the chapter referred to. n. stands for footnote.

WORKS OF MEREDITH
Mentioned, quoted, and discussed.

225

CHARACTERS IN MEREDITH'S STORIES

Mentioned or discussed.

Only such characters are listed as are sometimes referred to
out of direct connection with the work in which they appear.

AUTHORS

Books, and persons mentioned, with characters of fiction.